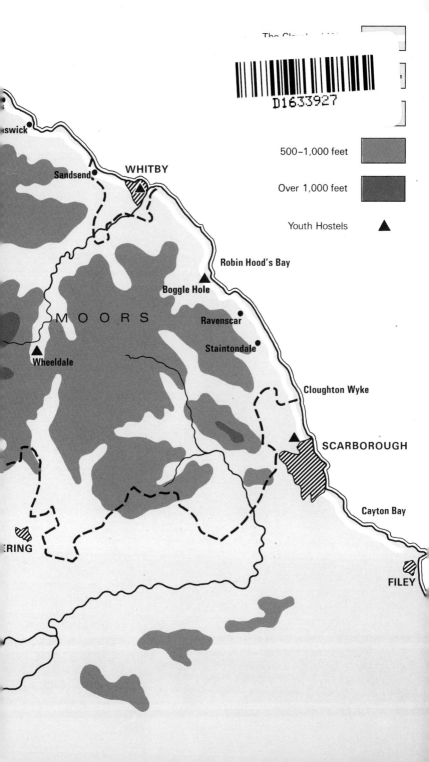

The Cleveland Way

500–1,000 feet	
Over 1,000 feet	
Youth Hostels	▲

D1633927

swick
Sandsend
WHITBY

Robin Hood's Bay

Boggle Hole ▲

M O O R S

Ravenscar

Staintondale

Wheeldale ▲

Cloughton Wyke

SCARBOROUGH ▲

Cayton Bay

ERING

FILEY

The Cleveland Way

Alan Falconer

Long-Distance Footpath Guide No 2

London Her Majesty's Stationery Office 1972

Published for the Countryside Commission

Pages vi and vii
Gormire Lake from Sutton Bank

The maps in this guide are extracts from
Ordnance Survey 1:25,000 (approximately
2½ Inches to 1 Mile) maps. They have
been prepared from production material
supplied by Ordnance Survey. Sheets
Nos. NZ40, 50, 51, 60, 61, 62, 71, 80, 81, 90;
SE48, 49, 58, 59, 68, 69, 89, 99; TA08

Drawings by Ronald Maddox

Wildlife drawings by Harry Titcombe

© Crown copyright 1972
Published by Her Majesty's Stationery Office

To be purchased from
49 High Holborn, London WC1V 6HB
13a Castle Street, Edinburgh EH2 3AR
109 St. Mary Street, Cardiff CF1 1JW
Brazennose Street, Manchester M60 8AS
50 Fairfax Street, Bristol BS1 3DE
258 Broad Street, Birmingham B1 2HE
80 Chichester Street, Belfast BT1 4JY
or through booksellers

Prepared for the
Countryside Commission by the
Central Office of Information

Printed in England for Her Majesty's Stationery Office
by W. S. Cowell Ltd, 8 Butter Market, Ipswich
iv SBN 11 700329 8   Dd 500042 K80

Maps

The waymark sign is used in plaque or stencil form by the Countryside Commission on long-distance footpaths

Preface

The Cleveland Way followed the Pennine Way in being officially opened as our second long-distance route. The Pembrokeshire Coast Path and Offa's Dyke Path have now been added, to give a total length of 678 miles. Others well on the way to completion are the South Downs Way and the Cornwall Coast Path.

The Cleveland Way is not the longest, but it is probably the most varied, with a backcloth ranging from fine coastal scenery to open moorland. Certainly, as Alan Falconer so well demonstrates, it lays bare, more plainly than any other, two hundred million years of the earth's history. It also takes the walker past countless sites of archaeological and historical interest, so that we read of life in the pre-Ice and Palaeolithic Ages, of Vindicianus, Harald Hardrada,

William the Conqueror, the Brus family, and Captain Cook, and of events right up to modern times. It has a full share of impressive landscapes, and Alan Falconer tells us where to look for birds and wild flowers.

The young and energetic will see in the peculiar weather a challenge, enabling them to test their orienteering skills in the remoter parts and to return home with a sense of achievement. The moorland and less frequented coastal stretches provide the solitude the town-weary need for refreshment. All will enjoy the bracing air and spaciousness which these historically rich coasts and uplands afford.

John Cripps
Chairman, Countryside Commission

Origins

To many walkers the Cleveland Way is merely the second of the Long-Distance Footpaths, of which the Pennine Way was the first; but the idea of a long holiday walk along the moors and cliffs goes back, in my infant recollections at least, to the summer of 1913 when my father went off on one of his usual Bank Holiday weekend treks. Starting from Saltburn, he set out along the escarpment to Osmotherley and on to Helmsley. Then, turning north again to Whitby, possibly using the old ridge road, known as Thurkilsty, to Round Howe, he followed the line of the Lyke Wake Walk to Wheeldale and then along Wade's Causeway. He came back by the coast, stopping to view the Roman camp recently investigated by his friend, William Hornsby of Saltburn.

It was, however, another close acquaintance, Frank Elgee of the local Dorman Museum, who suggested to my father the existence of a continuous "street" linking the coastal forts from Seaton to Scarborough and Filey. My father was also struck by an almost identical situation on the Hambleton Hills where two cliff forts, on Boltby Scar and Roulston Scar, were linked by a stretch of road marked as Cleveland Road, just as the lane near the Street Houses on Boulby Cliff was known as Cleveland Street.

It was much later when we learned that the Cleveland Street seemed to have been in continuous use from Roman times. Quarter Sessions' records, for instance, mention that the inhabitants of Skinningrove were fined for not repairing their section of the highway to Whitby, "known as the Middle Street, at a place known as Street Houses". Later, in 1655, the justices were still concerned that "the street on the coast between Boulby and Staithes was in great decay".

The existence of a long continuous Cleveland Road or Street was finally confirmed for us by the publication of Alfred Watkins' book *The Old Straight Track* in 1928. Watkins claimed that most of our ridge roads ran in a straight line from one landmark to the next. They had been surveyed in prehistoric times by expert "ley men" using poles which may have survived into the Middle Ages as "Palmers' walking staffs". According to Watkins, these primitive surveyors marked the ways with great stones, cairns and burial mounds on the headlands and ridges. They cut deep notches on the hillsides to mark where the ways climbed from the valleys, and used pools to reflect the line of march in the dales to the watchers on the hills.

Walkers on the Cleveland Way will have ample opportunity to test these theories of Alfred Watkins, or even counter with a few of their own. Why are some stones standing in line and others in triangular groups? Does a Christian cross beside an older monolith signify the adoption of Bronze Age tracks as medieval roads? Were burials made on the old highways because these were convenient assembly points to celebrate the burial of tribal chiefs? Whether or not you agree with Watkins you cannot but wonder at these and other possibilities as you pass the great howes or heaps of stones found on every ridge and headland along the Way.

After the founding of the Youth Hostels Association (England and Wales) in 1930, the Middlesbrough Rambling Club, of which my father was a founder member, saw the opportunity of promoting a long-distance holiday walk along the coast and cliffs, and enthusiastically supported the opening of hostels all along the route. Those at Stokesley, Osmotherley and Nether Silton did not long survive, however, and with the Way now established their loss is particularly felt.

It needed the glamour of the Pennine Way, together with the attendant publicity, to set the fashion for long-distance paths. We had to wait until the 1950s, but once the National Parks Commission gave its blessing to a long-distance Moors and Coast Path, the idea was taken up, often though with more vigour than wisdom before the exact route was decided. Arthur Puckrin, that notorious Lyke Wake Walk record-breaker, covered the Way in his seven-league boots in twice as many hours. I treasure particularly a report sent me by a group of works apprentices who "did" the Way in those uncharted days; some seem to have relied on maps attached to local bus timetables, travelling the roads along the foot of the hills. I quote some of their comments, though not wishing to spread undue alarm among prospective Wayfarers.

"In Oak Dale care should be taken as there are many snakes in the undergrowth" seems to invite the inevitable corollary, "there is a mortuary at the bottom of this path". I was informed that "the chances of getting a camp site at Kepwick are slim as the natives are very unfriendly". In Staithes, however, "the local people are friendly and there is a good fish and chip shop".

The National Parks Commission and the local authorities took nearly sixteen years to plan the route. The most difficult problems were met with in the highly urbanised areas around Guisborough and Skelton. This is still the least attractive part of the Way, and Y.H.A. parties have been known to cut out this part of the walk and take a bus from Saltburn to Guisborough. Some local ramblers would have preferred the Way to sweep round this area in a wide arc; in fact, an early draft map shows the ancient Cass Rock Gate from Guisborough to the Black Howes on the Quakers Causeway, as part of the Way. It turned north along this paved trod to Mutton Scalp Lane, using woodland paths through Kilton and Loftus ravines to reach the Cleveland Street at Street Houses. This route is more picturesque and romantic than the one actually chosen, but the desirability of including the Saltburn Youth Hostel and Hunt Cliff was a decisive factor in the final choice.

The Way has been signposted by Richard Bell, National Park Warden, with help from the local youth and rambling clubs. Vandals and cliff erosion have taken their toll of the carved wooden signs but these are being supplemented by a white acorn sign on fences, stones and tree trunks, and a scheme is in hand for regular maintenance of the Way by voluntary groups. 3

How to do it

The final designation of the Cleveland Way was not completed until 1969 and the official opening was performed at Helmsley Youth Hostel in May of that year: in reality hundreds of individuals and groups had been using it for fifteen years and more.

There is no ideal way of completing the walk: this must remain a matter of individual preference. It can be covered in a series of weekend walks, using car or public transport to the starting points close to or on the Way. I must, however, warn strangers to the area that bus services are few and buses likely to become rarer still on the moorland section of the walk.

A regular train service, including Sundays in the summer months, runs between Ayton and Whitby, crossing the Cleveland Way at Kildale. Osmotherley has two separate bus services linking it with Teesside and Northallerton; the service through the Cleveland villages below the escarpment is subsidised by the North Riding ratepayers, as are the bus services along the coast between Whitby, Robin Hood's Bay and Scarborough.

To spend a couple of days at, say, Guisborough, Stokesley and Osmotherley, walking sections of the Way in different directions each day and returning to base by alternative routes, seems to me a most rewarding way of spending a fortnight's summer holiday. I do most strongly recommend this circular tour programme, since one can explore the hundreds of places of interest at leisure. After all, for the authentic, awe-inspiring view of the "Cliffland", one must get below the cliffs; only by walking in the parklands around Kilburn, 5

Gormire, Kepwick and Ingleby Arncliffe can one appreciate the grandeur of the rock faces of the Hambleton Hills. Indeed many of the routes described in the Dalesman guide book *Walking in Cleveland* were written with this particular object in mind.

Many walkers will settle for a week's trip in one direction or the other. I recommend Helmsley to Filey for several good reasons. The prevailing winds are westerly: the exception is usually from the north and it is better to have the wind at one's back as much as possible. On the whole the views seem so much more impressive when one is walking east and south.

There is another important consideration if public transport is used—far fewer passengers travel to the townships near Teesside from the west, and people make for the coastal resorts at the beginning rather than the end of the day, when you will be more likely to find a seat on a bus.

Accommodation is the most daunting problem for anyone wishing to cover the whole distance in one holiday period. There are Youth Hostels at Helmsley, Scarborough, Boggle Hole, Whitby, Saltburn, Westerdale Hall and Wheeldale, and an abundance of hotels and boarding houses on the coast, but between Guisborough and Osmotherley one sees hardly a single farmhouse.

There is at least a bed and breakfast spot for a very limited number in Kildale. The Ramblers' Association publishes a bed and breakfast guide which it does its best to keep up to date; it includes farms, cottages and boarding houses where Cleveland Wayfarers will be welcome.

Meadow pipit

Some advice

Compared with the Pennine Way, the Cleveland Way is less than half the distance and at all times is much closer to habitation. It therefore should not impose too great a strain on stamina and route-finding skills, especially since much of it is so well trodden. Nevertheless, it is advisable to take reasonable precautions even for a comparatively short journey over any part of the Way. Conditions underfoot are more likely to lead to accidents than any other factor. Much of the cliff section is over boulder clay which can be slippery, even in gorse or bracken. One may suddenly find oneself sliding on a sloping, greasy patch of ground, and older, less supple walkers run the risk of sprains to wrist or ankle, or even cracked bones.

Choice of footwear is therefore of paramount importance. The wearing of Commando or Vibram soles and boots which give support to the ankle, is advisable. I have been using gumboots with transverse ribs on sole and heel for a number of years, but they do not prevent lateral sliding of the feet on slippery surfaces, although offering ideal protection for splashing through waterlogged paths or fording streams. I have heard of walkers who used rubber-studded hockey or baseball boots. I used to swear by good nails until I found my feet getting increasingly sore on hard roads. As there are some quite long stretches of hard surface along the Way, most walkers, I think, will be best served by the Commando-type sole even though the spaces rapidly fill with mud, with reduced effectiveness against slipping.

In dry weather a young and agile person could cover the whole course wearing only shorts and gym shoes, risking no worse than minor scratches from gorse and 7 briars or possibly dusty shale which stings bare flesh when whipped up by the wind. Trousers would, of course, ward off these inconveniences—and an additional point to remember in view of the sudden cold rain squalls is that wool and worsted are warmer and safer than cotton jeans.

The weather, until about June, is subject to sudden and unexpected changes, as I explain in the next chapter. That extra pullover or two recommended for even the hardiest mountaineers is no less essential on Boulby and Ravenscar. Light plastic or nylon capes have been much in favour in recent years—they are waterproof and cheap and also cover one's rucksack. In addition I would always have a high-waisted pair of over-trousers in good quality nylon, not so much for protection against the north-easterly squalls as for wading through the tall grasses and bracken along the moor and coastal paths. It's astonishing what a drenching one gets from sodden bracken, following a light shower or heavy dew.

On the moorland stretches particularly, where hospitality may be some hours ahead, exhaustion and fatigue can spell danger. As a precaution, see that youngsters and older members of your party are not carrying too heavy a load. I have known walks brought to a virtual standstill by younger members having overloaded themselves with such things as extra blankets, an overcoat, spare pair of boots, supplies of tinned food, bottles of assorted drinks, even an old-fashioned tent complete with wooden pole and pegs. More often than not, it pointed to a fond mother's over-zealous concern for her precious offspring. The maximum load for a youngster should be less than a third of his weight—and remember, the heavier the weather, the heavier the load. Forty pounds is a sensible upper limit to set for a journey between the coastal Youth Hostels.

If one of the party does suffer a bad sprain or a broken bone, don't urge the victim to struggle gallantly on. There are two rescue parties operating in conjunction with the warden service: one specialises in coastal rescue and the other in finding the lost and transporting the lame on the moorlands. Addresses and telephone numbers of these services are given on page 134.

8   While it is not easy to get lost when the clouds are

high, when a typical Cleveland "roak" or fog (of which more later) comes down the moors present a challenge to even the most experienced Wayfarers. At least one member of the party should have a good compass and know how to use it. Accurate interpretation of the contours of O.S. maps should supplement compass directions.

In these days of Outward Bound Schools, Education Field Centres and orienteering clubs, it should be unnecessary to suggest that the leader carry a whistle and first aid kit, possibly also emergency rations—Kendal mint cake, glucose sweets or oatmeal biscuits—to keep the party happy in case mist calls a prolonged halt to the day's march; remember, it is better to give low cloud a chance to clear than plunge forward into a possibly dangerous unknown.

If there is an injured or exhausted companion to be looked after, modern medical opinion suggests that alcohol and rubbing to induce warmth are to be avoided at all costs. It seems a shame that the redoubtable St. Bernard with his cask of cognac should be relegated to a back seat, but hot sweet tea is better than brandy, and a couple of pullovers and a waterproof cape wrapped round an exhausted walker provide the best temporary comfort until the experts arrive to deal with casualties.

Youth Hostel at Helmsley

Rest in a sheltered spot in the lee of a wall or rock: a depression among bracken makes an excellent bed and a covering of dry bracken fronds adds extra warmth, especially in a snowstorm.

Finally, do remember, as this is the National Park with the lowest rainfall, fire risk is particularly great. Even in winter, dry bracken and grass are highly inflammable.

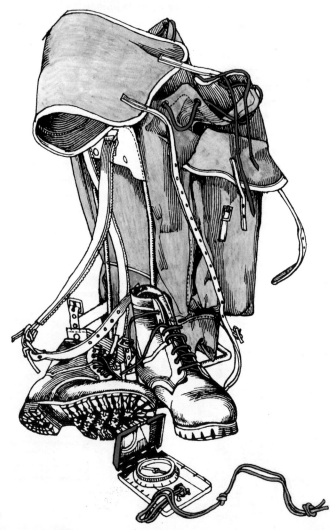

Weatherwise

One of the imponderables of the Way, of which walkers must be warned, is the local weather. Statistics show that the east coast is the driest part of England. Rainfall averages less than two inches per month compared with over ten inches in the heart of the Lake District or Snowdonia. But one must not be lulled into a false sense of security. Admittedly the moors and coastal cliffs do not get much rain, but it comes when least expected and with unusual severity. The old expression "a bolt from the blue", could so easily have originated in this part of the world where sudden thunderstorms develop rapidly on warm summer days. The root of these occasional troubles lies in two regional phenomena: first, the steep escarpment on the coast facing northeast and along the line of the Cleveland and Hambleton Hills overlooking the broad plains; secondly, the persistence of the polar air stream along the north-east coast. From Saltburn to Scarborough the cliffs turn to face this cold air stream, consequently throughout March and April, sometimes even in May and June, sudden showers of freezing hail or squalls of blinding, flurrying snow swirl around the high cliffs and moorlands as the cold blasts from the Arctic are forced upwards by the steep hills. Rapid freezing and condensation bring unexpected icy showers from bright skies.

But these occasional flurries of snow, above the national average perhaps on ten or twelve days, have their advantages. A fine powdering of snow fetches up the prints of long lost paths and dykes, especially in the early part of the year before the new season's grass and bracken have begun to sprout. I well remember being chased from the bleak escarpment by a wild north-easterly squall, dropping down from the Ingleby coal road near Burton Howe by the flagged path along Baysdale Middle Heads. Beyond the abbey I took the post- 11 man's path on the north side of the narrow valley and looked across at the southern bank just below the Gin Garth near Hob Hole. White streaks radiated like a huge spider's web from a small, grassy holm at the stream side. Why, I asked myself, should so many sunken tracks converge at so insignificant a spot? What could have created so many hollow ways? Later, after a summer excavation, the mystery was solved for me. Two iron-making bloomeries had operated here under the patronage of the nuns of Baysdale Abbey, the slopes of Baysdale were denuded of trees to provide the charcoal for the furnaces, and ironstone had probably come down the flagged path from an outcrop of Eller Beck ironstone near the three Burton Howes. This seam was re-opened in the mid-nineteenth century and the ore taken down an incline railway some distance from the better known Rosedale railway incline which the Cleveland Way crosses at Bloworth.

For many years Professor Gordon Manley and teams of young researchers at Durham University have made a special study of the North-East's weather. Some of his observations were published in a little pamphlet by the Royal Meteorological Society in 1935, which it is none too easy to come by nowadays. But no one who loves the open air can afford to be without Professor Manley's contribution to the New Naturalist series, *Climate and the British Scene*, a book which is not only fascinating but invaluable in helping ramblers and other outdoor lovers to anticipate weather and prepare accordingly.

One of the less pleasant characteristics of Cleveland weather, which affects these coasts and the ridges near the sea, is the notorious "roak", "sea fret" or sea mist. While the name "roak" is as old as the Vikings, I have yet to come across any reference which clearly distinguishes between the cloud banks, heavy with hail and snow, caused by the polar air in spring and early summer, and the entirely different phenomenon of the mid-summer fogs. These occur on warm quiet days with prevailing west winds of Force 2. The cold air from the sea begins to creep slowly in under the warm air over the land. All too often a low belt of fog is formed which blankets the coast in heavy drizzle. The temperature

drops twenty degrees or more. The cricketers of the county of broad acres know this trick of the weatherman only too well. How many dreary draws have Yorkshire endured at Hull and Scarborough while Sussex, Glamorgan and Kent raced to exciting victories on run-rich wickets on southern and western coasts!

Winds can become exceptionally strong as local conditions add their effect to the prevailing strength and direction. The top of Cringle Moor always seems to be lashed by winds three or four times the normal force. Westerly winds are channelled along the escarpment on the northern face as well as through the valleys and gaps to the south-west so that even on a day of moderate wind you can scarcely stand upright or make yourself heard near the look-out seat on the edge of this hill.

The steep escarpments reinforce thermal currents to the great advantage of glider pilots. It is enthralling on a warm summer day to sit watching the planes wheeling and turning over Whitestone Cliff or above Carlton Bank. Even when there seems to be hardly a breath of wind, the convection currents reach quite formidable strength, the faint drumming of the glider struts being the only sound in the quiet sky.

Gordon Manley is no believer in old wives' tales: he discounts the fisherman's dictum that the turn of the tide brings a change in the weather. But he does allow the possibility that where there is a broad stretch of sandy beach, the ebb and flow of the tide will affect cloud formation. A casual observer, which is all I can claim to be in this respect, would certainly find evidence to support this view. At ebb tide the broad sands at Teesmouth grow hot under the summer sun: the air clears, the sky becomes bright blue above the industrial haze of steel and chemical works. But when the tide flows, the cold air rushes across the estuary, the skies darken and a northerly squall brings notorious smog. Golfers, racegoers, cricketers and tennis players, no less than workers on the wharfside, know this phenomenon only too well. One may see the effect of wide, warm beaches even from a great distance. I have watched the clouds over the coast thirty or forty miles away and picked out the invisible headlands of Boulby, Ravenscar and Flamborough by the tall cumulus rising above them. Clear blue sky, in long stretches, marks the

Mulgrave, Robin Hood's Bay and Scarborough beaches with the warmer, drier air above them. I have no doubt that Hardrada and his experienced pilots made their landfall at Ravenscar by observation of the cloud pattern while still a hundred miles or more out at sea.

There is little question that the air along the coast is bracing. This does not necessarily mean windy and cold; and there is good scientific reasoning behind Cleveland's claim to its highly stimulating qualities. Variation is partly the key: changes in wind direction, force, temperature and humidity occur frequently, owing to the steep conformation of the cliffs and escarpments. The sensation on the skin is rather like the alleged effects of those bubble baths we see in commercial television. There are in fact invisible bubbles of damp air caressing and massaging our bodies as we walk through Cleveland's diverse airs on a day of sun and cloud.

Cleveland's weather makes our scenery too. The bare uplands, which contrast with some of the thickly wooded valleys, are due to the fierce squalls of our springs and winters. The few blackthorn bushes which border the cliff edge between Whitby and Cloughton lean over almost parallel to the ground in their efforts to escape the fury of winter's north-easters, and even the stray Corsican pines along the Roseberry Common escarpment seem to boast of branches only on the leeward side.

Geology

In 1933, Frank Elgee received an Honorary Doctorate from Leeds University for his lifetime research into the flora and fauna and archaeology of Cleveland, but he was accustomed to remark, with one of his rare smiles, that the North Yorkshire Moors were his university and the Cleveland Hills his particular college.

This remark is as profound as Elgee's wide research. Because of the bare nature of the uplands and the exposed strata on the coast, two hundred million years of the earth's history lie open for all to read.

Apart from the story of the rocks, every human culture from pre-Ice Age Palaeolithic through Neolithic, Bronze, Iron and Roman periods to medieval and modern times has left indelible marks and any observer may study them on the Way without straying more than a few yards from the designated line.

For the non-specialist it is a simple matter to visualise the formation of the North York Moors National Park. Take a thick slice of brown bread, top it with two slightly smaller wedges of red and white cheese and put the thick edge of the red cheese near the crusty top of the bread, placing the wedge of white cheese with its thick end just overlapping the pointed end of the red cheese. Cover the exposed areas of bread with a generous layer of butter. The bread represents the basic Liassic rocks of the Lower Jurassic period, which can be seen either in the valleys where the upper rocks have been cut away to expose the lower strata, or along the northeast edge of the area, that is the coast and cliffs. The butter obviously represents the greasy clays deposited by lakes and glaciers of the Ice Ages; the clay near the coast is boulder clay, the lacustrine clays are found in the Vales of Mowbray and Pickering.

Rising above the clays are the two wedges. The red
16 cheese stands for the long escarpment of the northern

coastal cliffs and the Cleveland Hills, which are mainly composed of Deltaic sediments overlain by sandstones. The white cheese further south shows us the long ridge of the Corallian limestones which run inland from the high perch of Scarborough Castle to the curve of the Hambleton Hills overlooking the Vale of Mowbray. Such a model is, of course, vastly over-simplified but it does enable the ordinary walker to understand the main features of the structure and scenery to be met with on the Cleveland Way.

Much of the Way is covered by the clays of the Pleistocene period, which for this purpose means Glacial period, although purists insist that the two terms are not interchangeable. The most important of the four Ice Ages was the last and, as our bread and butter model well illustrates, the Glacial clays and the last Ice Age made their marks mainly on the borders of the National Park, which the Cleveland Way follows fairly closely.

There were three great ice movements, during which the glaciers from the Pennines, the Cheviots and Scandinavia covered the slopes up to about eight hundred feet. Rough boulder clay from the Cheviot glacier covers most of the cliffs and the seashore and provides the green pastures which run to the very edge of the cliffs. Inland, the lower slopes of the hills were covered with rich alluvial clays which were extensively and profitably farmed once the natural forest was cleared, the marshes drained and efficient steel plough-shares adopted.

We can note the effects of the clay and ice, which dammed up the valleys and choked the preglacial river mouths, in this brief geological survey from Helmsley to Filey.

If you start your walk in Helmsley, you are made acutely aware of the Corallian limestones over the first few miles of the Way. The white cottages and field walls come from local limestone quarries which are still worked extensively. The soil is rich and provides good pasture and corn on the plateau on which the villages are built—you see them to the east of the Way —Scawton, Cold Kirby, Old Byland, and Murton.

Continuing along the Drove Road, one can trace the different texture and colour of the Upper Jurassic rocks 17

Helmsley Castle and Helmsley with Cleveland Way in foreground

in the worn surface of the road itself. Grey cornbrash and brown sandstones succeed the white ribbon of the earlier limestone track, just as the grass pastures give place to heather moor. As you drop down Oakdale and cross the Cod Beck, you are passing over the bed of an Ice Age lake and cannot fail to be impressed by the steepness and depth of this narrow valley, which was gouged out of surrounding rocks by the flood waters of melting ice which flowed down from the gap at Scarth Nick.

As the Way drops gently down from Scarth Nick to cross Scugdale, you pass through the long row of waste heaps left by the jet miners in the higher Lias strata. Beyond Scugdale stretches the main high ridge of the moors with their Middle Jurassic rocks—mostly sandstones and grits near the surface—the sand in particular is only too obvious where the Way skirts the bare glider

field; wind-blown sand drifts are already covering the heather on the north side. At both Carlton Bank and Hasty Bank there are other overflow channels for water impounded by the ice pack which reached a height of nearly eight hundred feet. The water flowed down Raisdale and Bilsdale, cutting a deep gorge into the Rye between Newgate Bank and Easterside Hill.

After crossing the main road at the top of Hasty Bank, the Lyke Wake Walk and the Cleveland Way run together across a short stretch of pasture on the south side of the forestry boundary. Walker-archaeologists will find much to interest them on the Way, but keen geologists will find more to their taste along the forestry tracks below the summit; two or three parallel rides pass round the natural bowl formed by the Ingleby re-entrant, known locally as Midnight. The foresters' bull-dozers have exposed the shales and clays; the fossils 19 which give their names to the various strata are frequently found hereabouts. If you do explore this scarp below Botton Head, you can return to the Cleveland Way by climbing the track of the old Rosedale railway incline to the ruined engine house which lies just below the Way at NZ609026.

Later, in crossing Kildale one can trace the developments of the Ice Ages once again. The river Leven left its bed in the centre of this broad dale and turned westwards, carving out a deep gorge along the northern edge of the ice and clay which filled the dale. This valley with its dark rocky walls can be followed by taking a woodland path, formerly a carriage drive from Kildale Hall, which leaves the Cleveland Way just below Bankside Farm.

Other deep channels worn by floods of Ice Age melt waters are seen at Gribdale Gate, below Roseberry Topping, flowing down Bousdale and, above all, in the narrow gap, Slape Wath, between Round Hill and Airy Hill where the Cleveland Way crosses the main Guisborough–Whitby road. Here again, as with the Leven, Boos Beck runs westward, reversing its natural course to the sea. Later, the Way recrosses this stream between Skelton and Saltburn where it sings its way through yet another Ice Age gorge below massive cliffs.

Along the cliff walk from Saltburn to Scarborough, one may see the whole of the Jurassic strata and the glacial drift exposed at one place or another. Owing to both vertical and lateral movement of great masses of rock in the Tertiary period, the earth seems to have opened up to reveal the secrets of its origins. This is particularly evident at Robin Hood's Bay and the Peak at the south end of the bay. The Upper and Middle Jurassic rocks have split and erosion has exposed the Liassic layers of the Lower Jurassic strata which are visible on the shore at low tide as well as in the base of the abandoned alum quarries.

On the cliffs at Ravenscar this great Peak fault leaves a steep face of about four hundred feet which has caused the Middle Jurassic Dogger layer to be exposed well below rocks of the earlier Middle Lias period. It is to Robin Hood's Bay and particularly the Ravenscar nature trail that school parties are taken to see the story unfolded by the rocks. The Lias are the oldest of

Cleveland Dyke with Roseberry Topping in the background

the Jurassic rocks, formed by mud and sand in open sea. There was considerable marine life, and fossils of ammonites, belemnites and lamellibranchs are found. In the ironstone seams even reptile fossils have been unearthed. About eight hundred feet of a total thickness of one thousand three hundred feet of Lower Lias is exposed on the shore and cliffs, and when viewed from the Ravenscar Hotel at low tide the curving scars have a curious wave-like appearance.

Above the Lias, the Middle Jurassic rocks tell the story of wide estuaries and deltas thrice covered by shallow seas which extended over a far wider area than the present National Park. The deltas abounded in plant life which later solidified into thin beds of coal. Some of these were worked—Graves' *History of Cleveland* mentions considerable activity in the late eighteenth century at the head of Baysdale not far from Burton Howe. Today the Cleveland Way uses the former 21

Ingleby coal road over Rudland Rigg.

It was probably during the third period of marine inundation that the Scarborough beds were laid down, to become the chief constituent of the high points of the moors from the coast at Hundale Point to Botton Head. Their sandstones ensured a good supply of water and the farmsteads and hamlets on the slopes are ranged along the spring line below. Above the farms the acid soils account for the blasted heath whose purple covering may be attractive but is none the less unproductive.

The Upper Jurassic rocks, which were also laid down in shallow seas, left some soft sandstones such as the Kellaways rock which has resisted erosion in isolated hill caps at Roseberry Topping and Freeborough Hill. But the main deposit of this period is the Corallian limestone belt already noted on the Hambleton Hills. These shell-based limestones, which combined with the coral reefs of a semi-tropical sea, survived erosion only in the southern part of the Cleveland Way. There was formerly a deep covering of Kimmeridge Clay and some Cretaceous chalk, but wind and rain have swept all traces of these deposits from the northern uplands, though the chalk still covers the Yorkshire Wolds and the cliffs south of Filey.

Most of the higher rugged cliffs between Scarborough and Hunt Cliff are capped with durable sandstones which frequently overhang the softer shales below: this accounts for the occasional severe cliff falls so characteristic of this coast. In the winter of 1969 keepers at Saltwick lighthouse were roused by a loud crack: subsequent inspection by Trinity House surveyors revealed fissures in the sandstone cliffs. Falls could occur following severe frost or heavy rain.

An interesting feature of the coast between Ravenscar and Cloughton is the terraced effect created by rock falls. The terraces support considerable vegetation and, in particular, masses of blackthorn and gorse sometimes obstruct the path. Another feature of the coast which derives from the Ice Age is the large number of narrow "groves", "graves" or "griffs" which drain the shallow basins of the hinterland and join together to erode a single deep outlet into the sea. The original

Section through Roseberry Topping, NNW to SSE

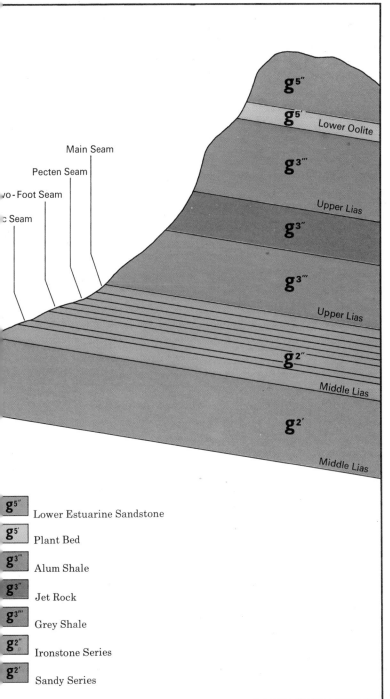

Main Seam

Pecten Seam

vo-Foot Seam

c Seam

g⁵″ Lower Oolite

g⁵′

g³‴ Upper Lias

g³″

g³‴ Upper Lias

g²″

g²′ Middle Lias

Middle Lias

g⁵″	Lower Estuarine Sandstone
g⁵′	Plant Bed
g³‴	Alum Shale
g³″	Jet Rock
g³‴	Grey Shale
g²″	Ironstone Series
g²′	Sandy Series

c

Lower Lias scars, Robin Hood's Bay

mouths of the streams were dammed up by the ice and boulder clay so that melt water from the moors burst new outlets at Skinningrove, Staithes, Sandsend and Whitby. The streams south of Whitby were turned south and west to seek the Ouse and Humber along the Vale of Pickering.

From Scarborough to Filey, most of the higher cliffs are capped by oolitic limestones of the Corallian series which overlie Oxford Clay. Scarborough's Castle Rock and Red Cliff at the south end of Cayton Bay provide excellent exposures, but Filey Brigg is obviously the most interesting formation. From Gristhorpe, the Calcareous Grit slopes gently down to sea level to form the long low ness of the Brigg. Unfortunately it is almost impossible to explore the cliffs from the shore and Wayfarers must be content to observe the pheno-menon from the cliff edge path.

For the geologist the coastal path and the shore below are a veritable outdoor museum. In a pocket guide such as this, one can only hope to arouse curiosity and direct it to other easily available sources of information. A booklet describing the geology of the Ravenscar nature trail can be bought at the Raven Hall Hotel or from local stationers. For the specialist, the Geologists' Association has a more detailed *Geology of the Yorkshire Coast (No. 34),* containing many long and difficult Latin names but also simple sketches of shore and cliff rock formations.

A very special geological feature is crossed by the Cleveland Way. This is the Cleveland or Whinstone Dyke. At some time in the Tertiary period when the major rock movements were taking place in Scotland, a massive narrow wedge of volcanic rock thrust through the upper layers of the earth's crust to form a 25

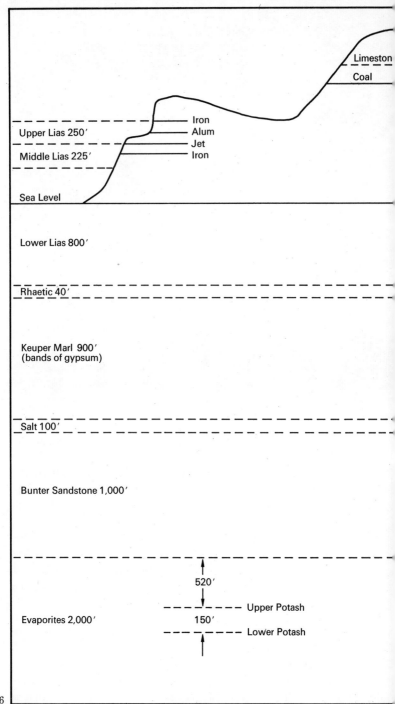

Limeston[e]

Coal

Iron

Upper Lias 250′

Alum

Jet

Middle Lias 225′

Iron

Sea Level

Lower Lias 800′

Rhaetic 40′

Keuper Marl 900′
(bands of gypsum)

Salt 100′

Bunter Sandstone 1,000′

520′

Upper Potash

Evaporites 2,000′

150′

Lower Potash

long dyke, which reaches the coast at Ravenscar. It rises abruptly from the clay soils of central Cleveland in the Langbargh Ridge between Ayton and Newton-under-Roseberry Topping and continues eastwards down Lonsdale towards Goathland and Ravenscar. This blue basaltic rock was very extensively quarried, being used in the construction of many of the local pack-pony causeways, some of which are still in reasonable condition; locally these are known as Pannierman's Trods or Saltergates. The so-called granite sets of many northern tramways came from the Cleveland quarries, and at Gribdale Gate the Leeds Tramway Company had a large quarry and private railway to ensure regular supplies of whinstone. The deserted quarries have filled with water to become picturesque "blue lagoons" into which adventurous youngsters launch themselves, using the quarry walls as high diving platforms. One of the finest lies close to the Way at the head of Lonsdale: when I plumbed its depths in 1925, I recorded fifty-seven feet of water, adequate, I imagine, for any diver.

Equally exciting are the "windy pits" of Ryedale, deep fissures and caverns in the porous and soluble rocks of the Corallian limestone. Currents of air build up deep underground and are blown out of the narrow obstructed mouths of the caves—hence their local name. The Ryedale caverns are not nearly as impressive —or commodious—as the potholes of Ingleborough or Clapham but archaeologists have explored them with great satisfaction, albeit considerable discomfort.

Bones of mammoth, rhinoceros and other sub-tropical fauna have been found in local caves—notably at Kirkdale, a tributary a mile or so lower down Ryedale than the starting point (or terminus, as the case may be) of the Cleveland Way at Helmsley. Man could have lived under these conditions but there is no evidence of his having used the caves before the Ice Ages. There is, however, ample proof of continual usage over the past four thousand years. Excavation has shown that caves and windy pits were used for urn burials, Neolithic orgies and as medieval rubbish dumps. The most recent excavation uncovered bottles, tins and other twentieth-century garbage from the war years when Polish troops were encamped in nearby Duncombe Park: you see the concrete foundations of their Nissen huts as you climb out of the first gill to be crossed after leaving Helmsley.

And thereby, as they say, hangs a tale. In 1940 the Helmsley folk warmly welcomed the refugee Poles who were quartered in the woods above the old castle. They were privileged to share the inadequate supplies of beer and spirits in the local inns and to supplement their rations of spam and dried egg with coarse fish from Ryedale's many streams. All was serene until one balmy summer's evening when Janek, a Polish warrior, was trailing his line in the deep pool near Helmsley bridge. He was not to know that here was the home of

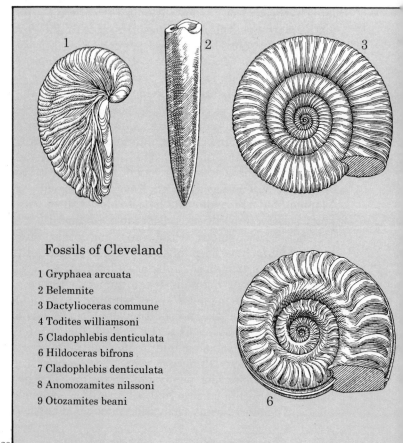

Fossils of Cleveland

1 Gryphaea arcuata
2 Belemnite
3 Dactylioceras commune
4 Todites williamsoni
5 Cladophlebis denticulata
6 Hildoceras bifrons
7 Cladophlebis denticulata
8 Anomozamites nilssoni
9 Otozamites beani

Hercules, the giant trout, Helmsley's pride, accustomed to feed on the offals from the butcher's shop until war-time scarcity restricted his supplies. Which could explain why Hercules took the austere bait offered by Janek, and met his end from a stout pair of Army boots. Proudly Janek carried his prize into the local beer parlour. His offer to share the coming feast with his Helmsley friends was met with an icy silence. Henceforward innkeepers stopped "the Poles' tap" and they were forced to retire to the windy pit at Antofts, just across the Rye from their camp, where their empty wine bottles added to the debris choking the entry to the cavern. The determination of a group of Ampleforth schoolboys led to the opening of the pit and the discovery of its prehistoric treasures.

TEESSIDE

Guisborough

Bo
Do

Cleveland

Cleveland
Dyke

Cleveland
Dome

Osmotherley

Helmsley

Thirsk

▬ ▬ ▬ National Park
Boundary

— ∙ — ∙ — Fault

Kimm
Clay

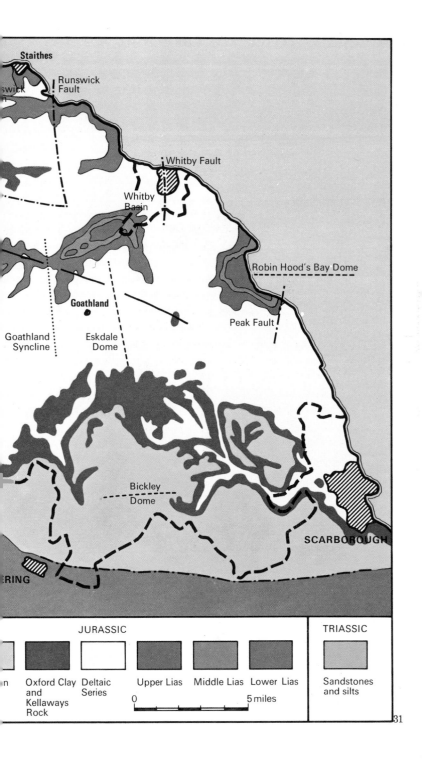

Plants and birds

Bird's-eye primrose

The North Yorkshire Moors and their valleys have been a veritable goldmine for botanists. Over the years collectors have been digging up rare plants, in some cases even offering their spoils for sale. It was inevitable that the area should become famed for its beauty, once Wordsworth and the Lake Poets made nature fashionable. Although the poet and his sister came on a visit, and much to the astonishment of their saucy hostess of the "Three Tuns" at Thirsk, left their postchaise to walk to Helmsley, Dorothy's *Journal* is singularly unrewarding about the event. Her darting eyes noticed only the most prosaic details such as the little Scottish cattle panting their way along the Drovers Road. She looked at the "curious stone" near Sutton Bank but failed to see the Devil's Footprint on its face. She saw the townships which dotted the landscape below the hills but missed the wonderful view, so beloved of modern photographers, of Gormire. She remarks on the bread and milk at the "Sportsmen's Inn" (now "The Hare") at Scawton but mentions only one flower (wild rose) and one birdsong (thrush).

A later diary of a walk along the Cleveland Way is given in Edmund Bogg's *Charm of the Hambletons*. He and the Thirsk naturalists could count as many as one hundred and sixty herbs in a single afternoon's walk up Sneck Yate, above Boltby, and I can confirm the wealth of flowers still to be seen there. Bogg also records almost two hundred different birds, residents or visitors to the area. Besides the havoc wrought by modern pesticides, weed killers and fertilisers, other factors such as afforestation and deforestation, drainage of marshlands and the spread of bracken have radically altered the ecology of the land. But it is the deliberate vandalism of collectors which is responsible for the loss of the rarest plants.

Bogg mentions a large number of herbs which were much prized in his time, before State medicine gave us packaged drugs free of charge (well almost!). Elderflower and berry provided soothing syrups; gout weed relieved that painful complaint; the plentiful celandine gave a juice that cured spots on the eyes; strong scented lettuce was a substitute for opium; scurvy grass was an anti-scorbutic; and soapwort had an obvious use. The centaury and the gentian were prized as appetisers and the deadly nightshade used with caution by homeopaths.

The Hambleton Hills are still a mecca for the naturalist: the Way goes through two nature reserves—near Ashberry Farm at Rievaulx and above Gormire where there is a nature trail. On the coast there is a reserve at Hayburn and a trail at Ravenscar.

Because of the rich diversity of rocks, as noted in the previous chapter, the Way provides a great variety of plant life. Plants are most profuse in the limestone valleys although there is less tree and hedgerow shade than there used to be. Spurge laurel and violets of every kind, even the rare hairy violet, may be seen in the valleys. Stinking hellebore and the blue and red cranesbill are still thriving. The soil, as one climbs towards the higher slopes of Black Hambleton, becomes sandier and more acid, the flowers rarer, the most common being the tormentil, heaths and bedstraw. A few very rare flowers are being preserved in the Ashberry nature reserve such as the bird's-eye primrose, globe flower and white bogbean. Orchids particularly suffer because they do not survive picking, like bluebells near which they are often found.

The moors, however, do not offer a great wealth of flowers and the spread of bracken threatens even the few hardy perennials that show themselves. It is a different story when we reach the coast where flowers flourish in abundant variety in the clay soils. The best pockets are found in the deep valleys that run down to Saltburn, Staithes, Sandsend and Hayburn Wyke. There is abundance of colour at all times of the year except winter. The common flowers such as primrose, bluebell, harebell, cowslip, clover and vetch hardly need mention, but there are also other more interesting specimens to delight even the most ardent naturalist: wild thyme, small scabious, salad burnet, spotted orchids and the attractive wood vetch; added to which are: everlasting pea, Bythinian vetch (a rare one this) and bee orchids.

Flowers are to be found in the old rail cuttings and mine workings, where they have perhaps strayed from former cottage gardens. I noted a long stretch of valerian in the Sandsend area, and near the old line on Huntcliff

I failed to identify a patch of blue flowers which could

Black-headed gull and herring gull

have been degenerate delphiniums. At Cowbar I almost confused wood mallow with the meadow cranesbill of the Hambleton lanes, but an old miner suggested that the plants had come from local flower beds levelled to make room for garages.

Even more than flowers, bird life has decreased in recent years. I have not seen a buzzard hereabouts since 1954. Herons, which used to fish in the Rye, seem to have been driven elsewhere. On the coast the diving birds seem fewer at every visit although the Tees' mouth is still a popular haunt for migrating species. As many as twenty thousand birds can be seen feeding on the sands and marshes on a single afternoon. Some of the rarer visitors may occasionally be seen farther south, and on the sands and cliffs the tern is most likely to be met with.

Most of us, however, will be content to be able still to listen to the full chorus of bird cries. Like the fine lady on her way to Banbury Cross, we shall have music wherever we go: curlew, peewit and lark on the heathland; warbler, thrush, wren and blackbird in the woods; chatter of finch and linnet in the hedgerows; but, alas, no corncrake any more in the ploughland and high meadows.

Female emperor moth and caterpillar on ling

Man and Cleveland

Preglacial times

Although many of the higher moorlands were untouched by the great glaciers of the Ice Age, there is little now left on our moors to indicate that men inhabited the Cleveland Hills in preglacial times. The bones of hyena, soft-nosed rhinoceros and other fauna associated with a warm climate have been found in the area. Man could certainly have maintained a reasonably comfortable existence alongside them. As the climate grew colder, and the mammoth and woolly rhinoceros, with their warm hairy hides, replaced the earlier sun-loving creatures, man probably fled southwards.

The most remarkable finds of preglacial animal bones come from the Kirkdale Cave (SE678856), some six miles east of the start of the Cleveland Way. Other similar caves in Ryedale have yet to be thoroughly explored and undoubtedly there are more caverns to be discovered.

Although no artefacts of Palaeolithic man have been found on the present line of the Cleveland Way, Frank Elgee unearthed a crude stone implement, some four and a half inches long, below the site of a Neolithic camp on Eston Beacon, a landmark visible from almost any point on the escarpment of the Cleveland Hills.

Pygmy flint man 6000–2000 B.C.

Perhaps as early as 6000 B.C., men using "pygmy" flints braved the tundra conditions which succeeded the Ice Age. After heavy showers of rain or heath fires, you may be lucky enough to catch the gleam of a particle of pale grey flint on the yellow-brown sandstones of the high moors. Shepherds, keepers and amateur archaeologists have picked up flint chippings by the bucketful and finds are still made regularly by observant walkers. 37

Many of the chips are obviously waste material since the art of flint making was not so well developed at this early stage. Sometimes the finds have been so numerous and concentrated as to warrant the theory that they came from flint tool factories. Dr. and Mrs. Frank Elgee put forward the suggestion, which has not, however, found universal favour. Quite independently, I was led to the same conclusion from my experiences of a site on the slopes of White Gill not far from Burton Howe.

There are certain places on the Way where it may pay one to keep an eye open for flints: near Sneck Yate (SE508878) on the Hambletons; almost anywhere on Whorlton Moor; Carlton Moor, especially near Thackdale Head (NZ519025); over a wide area of Botton Head on the bare patches surrounding the concrete trigpoint; and at Burton Howe (NZ608033). These tiny scraps of flint are not readily recognisable as implements: they are more like broken teeth and were fitted into wood or bone shafts to make sickles, knives and saws. The serrated iron sickle, used later in North Yorkshire, was perhaps a copy of this earlier Mesolithic pattern.

3000–1000 B.C.

Although I have given approximate dates for prehistoric periods, the communities belonging to different cultures demonstrably lived alongside each other and there is considerable overlapping of the successive ages.

The Neolithic era is distinguishable from the earlier Mesolithic by several features. The men of the New Stone Age cultivated emmer wheat and "naked" barley, that is, barley without its characteristic beard. They buried their dead in long barrows surrounded by ditches, possibly keeping the corpses for some time before collective burial.

Neolithic stone axes were made from basalt, whinstone and sometimes ironstone. Many came from the Borrowdale and Langdale factories in the Lake District, which obviously necessitated a well-marked cross-country route. The passage from the Pennines to the Neolithic settlements of the Blackamoor seems to have followed the Morainic ridge of the Ainsty, using the

line of the Drove Road over the Hambletons. Two extensive long barrows have been excavated on the Hambletons, one near Wass (SE563802) and the other close to the Cleveland Way above Kepwick (SE492903).

Perhaps it was these folk who established the tradition of the Lyke Wake Walk. According to Elgee, they probably kept their dead until the flesh had rotted from the bones because they believed the stench of decaying flesh to be offensive to their gods. The fragmented bones would be buried at a mass funeral ceremony, the custom and manner of burial deriving from eastern Mediterranean sources.

Late Neolithic flint implements are not nearly so easy to come by as the Mesolithic hoards, but as recently as the summer of 1970 a casual walker on Carlton Bank Top picked up a delicately flaked, tanged and barbed arrowhead, quite one of the most beautiful I have ever seen. I have a similar purple-grey flint found near the huge howe on Botton Head in 1961.

Bronze Age 2000–300 B.C.

When we come to the Early Bronze Age, which overlaps the late Neolithic, we find many and more authentic relics of the people who inhabited the high moors. Bronze Age round barrows cover many of the ridges and south-facing slopes. The largest burial mounds are found on ridge-crests; those on the Cleveland Way are to be seen at Drake Howe (NZ537029) on Cringle Moor, and the huge barrow mentioned previously on Botton Head (NZ594016). A tumulus of a very different kind, known as Three Lords' Stone, is on the top of Carlton Bank just below Drake Howe, and a group of four tumuli (Burton Howe) lies close to the Way on the Rudland Rigg road (NZ608033). These tumuli not only marked the line of ancient ridge roads, they were later adopted as parish and manorial boundaries by Theodore of Tarsus and the Domesday surveyors respectively. The tumulus on Drake Howe is referred to as Odin's Cave in a boundary survey in the Feversham estate records in 1642.

It was during the Bronze Age that many of the long clefts or dykes were hewn out of the moor floor. The Cleveland Way runs parallel to the Cleave Dyke for two miles or more on Hambleton Moor, and an elaborate Bronze Age fortified camp can be traced on Boltby Scar 39

D

Wade's Causeway, Wheeldale Moor

(SE506857). Near this fort the Hesketh Dyke runs at right angles to the Cleave Dyke. Another dyke starts just south of the Cleveland Way on Hasty Bank but turns south along the western scarp of Urra Moor.

The Way crosses another dyke, marked as the War Dyke, just north of Beast Cliff (NZ995000). This dyke has almost disappeared under the plough, but compared to the other dykes it is shorter, probably of later date and was made for a different purpose. I shall refer to it later in the guide in connection with Harald Hardrada and the Viking invasions.

The reason for the long dykes remains a mystery. They were originally composed of a wall of natural boulders overlooking a ditch eight or ten feet deep.

They may have been defensive, but where would the sparse population of those early civilisations find the numbers to man them effectively? A number of these earthworks are known as "park" dykes, which suggests they formed enclosures for wild animals—the animals being driven into the ditches by beaters and despatched by the spearmen on the walls. Or perhaps they served as a formidable obstacle to cattle raiders. Again, they may have marked out tribal boundaries; they certainly came to be used as such by the monks. The Rievaulx cartulary, for instance, refers to the land *infra fossatum* which the monks held as a gift from Robert de Mainil in Ingleby (Greenhow). In 1642 the survey of the Helmsley estates also refers to the Urra Moor dyke— the Helmsley boundary ran along the "street" leading to Stokesley as far as the Cliff Dyke on Urra Moor.

Great Ayton Moor has dozens of small tumuli dating from the Bronze Age—a veritable necropolis or city of the dead. There are two or three excavated sites close to the Way which have not yet been satisfactorily explained, and early in the year, before the bracken gets too high, much of the detail is fairly easy to distinguish. The first is a tomb with a long serpentine tail of stones stretching away to the north from a mound that contained several burial "kists" formed from roughly squared stone slabs. The second is about a quarter mile farther east—a rectangular enclosure defended by rampart and ditch. I had always thought that it must have been a temporary camp for a Romano-British posse probably chasing rebels or rustlers, but local archaeologists date it much earlier.

Although the round barrows are associated with the Bronze Age period, most of the burial artefacts found have been of flint because bronze was scarce and largely monopolised by the more prosperous communities on the Yorkshire Wolds. Pottery and beads, however, have been unearthed and the men who lived along the Way in the Bronze Age are often referred to as Beaker folk or Urn people. They could almost certainly weave and may have lived in pit huts, although the only hut sites I have seen near the Way, at Percy Cross (NZ606118), date from the very short period of the Iron Age, which in north Yorkshire began about 250 B.C. and soon gave place to the Roman era.

41

The Romans in the North-East

The weather of our North-East coast, the inhospitable nature of the moorland and the poverty of the primitive hill communities must have held little attraction for the conquerors from sunny Italy. It was not until the legions were almost on the point of withdrawing under repeated threats of invasion all along the northern and eastern boundaries of their empire that they began to make more or less permanent structures near the Cleveland Way. Later, in the fourth century, they appointed a Count of the Saxon Shore and built a line of small forts with high wooden watch towers from the Tees Bay to Filey, linked by the Cliffland (or Cleveland) Street, mentioned earlier.

Hornsby's excavations suggested the late fourth century as the possible date of the Roman fortifications. This is confirmed by an inscription on a stone at the Ravenscar camp: "Vindicianus, prefect of the soldiers, built this camp when Justinian was the commander". Since Justinian returned to Gaul in A.D. 407, the date of the camp seems to be fairly accurately fixed. This same Vindicianus must have lived in the area for some considerable time, as a tombstone, found in 1640 near East Ness, but now lost, was inscribed: "Valerius Vindicianus had this tomb made for his wife Tibia Pinta, aged 38, his sons Valerius, aged 20, and Variolus, aged 15".

When the legions were finally withdrawn in A.D. 410, the Saxon and Scots invaders overran the forts, burned the towers and threw the mutilated bodies of the guards and their families into the wells. Today only the site of the fort on Castle Hill, Scarborough, is worth inspection. The camps were linked with Malton, the garrison town, by a road built much earlier. It became known in later times as Wade's Causeway, and part of it has been excavated and maintained by the Ministry of Public Building and Works (now incorporated in the Department of the Environment) on Wheeldale Moor near Stape. Wade's identity remains something of a

Top right: Plan of Roman (late 4th century) coast defence blockhouse and signal station. (Reproduced by courtesy of Methuen & Co. Ltd.)

Bottom right: Stone found at Ravenscar, records building of a coast-guard fort by Vindicianus

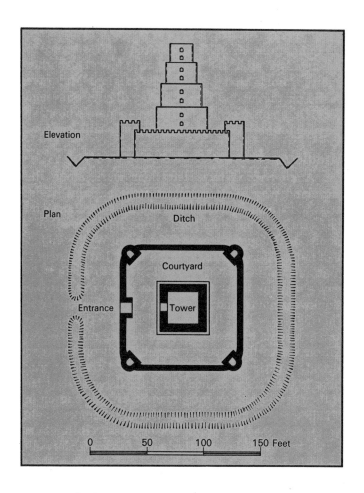

Elevation

Plan

Ditch

Courtyard

Entrance   Tower

0   50   100   150 Feet

mystery. Some historians believe he was a Briton who, as Count of the Saxon Shore, offered stiff resistance to the invaders after the Roman withdrawal. Another tradition holds that he built the original Mulgrave Castle on the mound in the deep valley of Sandsend Beck. Or, again, legend has it, he was a giant who made the road for his wife to cross the moor to milk her cow.

Middle Ages

The Anglo-Saxons have left their mark along the Cleveland Way in no uncertain fashion. Saint Hilda, it is said, turned all the snakes into stone, and you may still pick up their curly stone relics (fossil ammonites) all along the coast. The present Whitby Abbey is of much later date than Saxon times but the monks continued to use the Cleveland Street to make their way along the coast to the sister abbeys at Jarrow, Monkwearmouth and Lindisfarne. They had a cell at Thorfilda, now East Row at Sandsend, on the site of a former temple to Thor. A second resting place was at Kilton where there was a hermit's cell on the road already mentioned as Middle Street. Farther north, close to the Tees, a foundation still existed at the time of the Dissolution, on the site of St. Hilda's church in Middlesbrough market place. Here the monks would wait to ford the river at low tide or cross to Billingham Creek by the Bishop of Durham's ferry. Hinderwell, formerly St. Hilda's well, was obviously another place of rest and refreshment.

When the Danish invaders came they settled down alongside the earlier Anglian immigrants. In nearly all the parishes below the Way which bear the Anglian names by which they were known when Theodore of Tarsus first organised the parish system in the late seventh century, we still find a Danish village. Hutton and Rudby are now one village, so are Kirkby and Broughton. Thornaby and Thornton, Stainsby and Stainton are settlements on either side of Stainton Beck where the Danes occupied the land near the Fleet or tidal water, while the Angles lived farther up the stream. The Way also goes close above Easby and Ayton. Later it passes through Anglian Hinderwell and Norse Runswick, Goldsborough and Kettleness, Cayton and Osgodby. Most interesting, perhaps, is the

village of Swainby, which became the senior partner in the parish of Whorlton when the population around the church and castle was wiped out by the plague.

Scandinavian words still survive in moorland dialect: "grain" is a branch, "ness" a headland, "beck" a local word for stream, and "roak" is our own peculiar mist or fog.

Not much remains of Danish origin along the Way, although there are some fine crosses and hog-back tombs in churches on the plain. A fine hoard of Viking armour found in Kildale Church was stolen in the late nineteenth century. It included swords, two-edged daggers, iron axeheads, buckles and even a pair of scales, an indication that the Vikings were part warriors, part merchants.

Bankside Farm, in Kildale, through the farmyard of which the Cleveland Way passes, is built on the plan of the Danish long house, in which the ten dozen warriors of a Danish "hundred" would range themselves on each side of the long hearth stretching the whole length of the house. Such a meeting was a Hus Thing where every man could have his say. Larger Things were held out of doors on prominent hills. If you look down from the top of Easby Moor to the south of the monument to Captain Cook, you should see the clump of trees on a knoll where the Thing of the Wapentake of Langbargh met. The Balliols were later to use this site for their castle.

For a time Norman tyranny destroyed this democratic way of life but it was the men of Cleveland who won back their ancient liberties from King John; Ros of Helmsley, Brus of Skelton, and Percy of Kildale were the leaders who forced John to promise no tax should be imposed without the consent of the Common Council.

The Anglian and Danish civilisations fashioned a church which used the vernacular and allowed marriage of clergy. Such liturgical innovation was nipped in the bud with the coming of the Normans as emissaries of the Pope in 1066. But it was a humble tenant of the Balliols, John Wiclif, "the morning star of the Reformation", who in the closing years of the fourteenth century, from the Oxford college founded by his patrons, reintroduced the Gospels in English.

It is on the headland of Ravenscar, however, that the

Bankside Farm, Kildale, built on the plan of the Danish long house

Viking reverberations are felt at their strongest. Here the Raven banner, emblem of the "Landwaster", was first planted. A mile to the south the War Dyke crosses the line of the Way, while to the west is the Green Dyke. Between these flamed the beacon which guided the raiding fleets to this traditional assembly point. The raiders sheltered in the Danes Dale behind the twin dykes; a small guard was left to protect the long ships while the main body pillaged the countryside.

Hardrada landed here before he faced Harold Godwinson at Stamford Bridge and duly took up Harold's offer of six good feet of English ground. In the saga of Harald Hardrada we find the name "Cliffland" mentioned for the first time. One of Harald's counsellors warns him that the Thingmen in England would prove more than a match for his warriors, which tells us something of the fusion of Angle and Dane which must have come about by this time. Harald, however, was in no mood to listen to advice; not for nothing was he nicknamed Hardrada, "the man hard to advise". He had been everywhere and knew everything. In 1066 when he reached Scarborough he used a trick learned while fighting in the Eastern Roman Empire as a captain in the Varangian Guard; he set fire to the town by 46 hurling down burning brands from the cliff above. He had fired a fortified town in Sicily by enticing pigeons from the houses and releasing them with Greek fire attached to their legs. They returned to their nests in the thatched roofs with highly gratifying results. Hardrada had broken all records as a collector of treasure; some of the coins from Baghdad which were found in York must have come from the hoard he carried with him to win over the Jarls of northern Britain whose support he needed. The remarkable carvings in stone and metal, typical of Viking relics, show that they had learned much from the East and indeed surpassed the Normans in craftsmanship. Can we ever estimate England's loss through the destruction of these arts?

However, there is no denying that the North-East owes a tremendous debt to the monks who came with the Normans. Their magnificent abbeys—at Rievaulx, Byland, Guisborough, Whitby and Mount Grace—and the ruins of Norman castles at Helmsley, Whorlton, Skelton, Kilton, Mulgrave and Scarborough, testify to the dominance of the more sophisticated architectural styles from Europe over the old native methods of building. Splendid edifices, indeed, but at what cost in taxes to the Saxon peasantry!

I shall pass over those monuments that come under the care of the Department of the Environment, which also provides a series of excellent guides, but I must say a word or two about some of the lesser-known ruins to be found near the Way.

One of the rare fortified village sites is to be found at Whorlton. The Meynell family, Jew-baiters and boon companions to our more spendthrift kings, built their castle here in the twelfth century. There is a fine wooden carving on one of the tombs in the church of a Crusader, Sir Nicholas de Meynell, with his dog at his feet. You can hardly miss the avenue of yews but keep a look-out for the deep grooves in the walls where arrows were sharpened.

The stronghold of the Brus family at Skelton is probably better read about than visited. After King John had razed their castle at Danby, the family made their home at Skelton and made provision for their after-life by generous gifts to the Church. They promised a thousand haddocks from their fisheries at Coatham 47

Rievaulx Abbey

to the monks of Byland and no doubt used the Cleveland Way to deliver them. They founded Guisborough Priory and made available a forty-foot way, to be maintained by the Brus peasantry, for the use of the Austin Friars to transport their tithes of corn, cattle and sheep from Coatham and Upleatham. This paved trod can still be traced and was considered as a possible alternative to the present path through the alum wastes of Slape Wath.

48   The castles at Kilton and Mulgrave were built in the

early thirteenth century, probably in the troubled times of King John. Both show interesting developments of the period, being adapted to the narrow ridges on which they were built. They had defence in depth rather than the concentric fortifications developed in Edward I's time. Peter de Mauley was given the lands at Mulgrave for his part in the murder of Prince Arthur of Brittany, John's rival for the throne. Kilton was strengthened by a vassal of the Brus to counter the royalist bastion at Mulgrave. Eventually it passed to 49

Hand Stone on Urra Moor

the Thwengs by marriage to a Brus heiress. A member of the family, Lucia de Thweng, made a name for herself in the manner of the wife of Bath: besides husbands at church door, she enjoyed other company, notably that of Nicholas de Meynell. The novel *The Green Popinjays*, by Eleanor Fairbairn, is well worth reading as an interesting evocation of the particular period and place.

The Brus lords had right of wrack and warren, i.e. a sovereign's monopoly to wrecks and hunting, from Coatham to the Riding Stones at Kettleness. These stones are occasionally referred to as Wade's Stones or 50 Old Wives Stones, indicating, as Alfred Watkins claimed, the continuity of Stone Age marks down to modern times. The Brus' demesne coincided with the Wapentake set up by Halfdene, the Danish king of York, in the ninth century. The Earls of Mulgrave enjoyed similar privileges as far as East Beck, where the jurisdiction of Whitby Abbey began.

Besides its connections with the Brus family, Skelton has associations with another famous figure—the novelist Laurence Sterne. The author of *Tristram Shandy* was Rector of Coxwold and a popular visitor here. He loved a joke and is said to have invented the legend of how Thomas Challenor of Guisborough kidnapped the Italian alum workers of Puteoli in order to learn the secret of their art.

Laurence Sterne (1713–1768), from marble bust by J. Nollekens

Sailors and smugglers

No description of the Way would be complete without a reference to the most famous of all Cleveland Wayfarers, Captain James Cook, whose monument on Easby Moor is the most prominent landmark on the route. Australian visitors in particular are eager to see the places and objects connected with the great voyager. The schoolroom at Great Ayton, where he learned navigational mathematics, houses a small museum. His home, clearly visible from Roseberry Topping, lies close below the Way, a quarter mile to the south, at Airy Holme. No doubt he travelled the Cleveland Way to his first apprenticeship at Staithes and may well have echoed the concern of the justices in 1655 at the decay of the street. Returning from Whitby to visit his parents in Ayton, he would probably follow the street as far as Staithes and then work his way up the Ridge Lane of the smugglers to the moors, where a track led across to the ancient White Cross at Commondale. He might have then taken the way by the Black Howes to Highcliff, once suggested as a line for the Cleveland Way. There are statues and plaques in Whitby, pictures and charts in the Pannett Park library there to tell you more about Cook, the bicentenary of whose discovery of New Zealand the town celebrated in 1970.

A visitor about as welcome, but perhaps not quite so destructive as the Vikings, was the privateer commanded by Captain Paul Jones during the American War of Independence. A less famous but more acceptable local hero was Captain Constantine Phipps, later Earl of Mulgrave, who in 1773 sailed for the North Pole in the ketch *Racehorse*. Like Captain Cook, Phipps was accompanied by a number of distinguished scientists and they made valuable observations, though not

of course on anything like the same scale as Cook and

his team in the South Seas. Phipps fought with distinction in the American War, principally at the battle of Ushant (1778).

Smuggling was the main activity along the coast, and the legends which recount the intrepidity of the "gentlemen" and the helplessness of the coastguards are endless. The landed gentry of the district seem to have put up much of the capital for the rum and tobacco runners. The headquarters of the notorious John Andrews was the "Old Ship Inn" at Saltburn. His activities were on a scale and in the style of an American bootlegger of the 1920s. Robin Hood's Bay was the centre of the traffic, owing to its remoteness, and tales are still current of how the smugglers passed goods and bodies from house to house under the noses of the coastguards and Revenue officers. In the autumn of 1970, in the course of an afternoon I heard two stories of underground passages into which farm tractors had fallen. These were of course smugglers' tunnels and not, as I had imagined, old half-filled dykes or alum and iron workings. There is a charming little book on Robin Hood's Bay by Barrie Farnill, which I recommend to anyone who wants to get the most out of his trip along the Way.

Backstaff, forerunner of the sextant, for determining latitude at sea, in use when James Cook was in his apprenticeship at Whitby

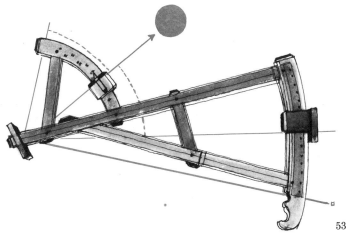

Alum, jet and iron

The reader may think it odd to find a chapter on local industries in a guide book dealing with a National Park area, but Cleveland industries have a unique local significance, and evidence of industrial activity almost forces itself on one's attention all along the route.

The oldest and most romantic of the Cleveland industries is undoubtedly jet mining. Ornaments of delicately carved Cleveland jet have been found associated with round barrow burials. As late as the 1860s a jet chain guard, four and a half feet in length, was ordered for the "Queen of Bavaria", or was it perhaps for the famous Lola Montez herself?

Jet was often among the mixed bag of oddments picked up by beachcombers along the sea-shore: these were known in my schooldays as "Klondykers" because they hoped to find an occasional gold coin dropped from a ship or a careless holidaymaker's pocket. In 1800, after a certain Captain Tremlett persuaded the jet workers to use lathes to turn the jet, the Whitby industry entered on a period of prosperity which reached boom proportions when Queen Victoria made the wearing of jet adornments a royal fashion after the death of Dear Albert. Some fourteen hundred men and boys were earning more than twice the national average wage by 1870; in spite of the dust and grime involved in the work, they were reputed to be very healthy.

The demand for jet was so great that mining operations were started on a commercial scale all along the line of the jet shales on the Cleveland escarpment. Jet miners' inns (Jeator House near Osmotherley was one) were not only used as miners' lodges but were meeting places for miner and merchant. There were three inns in the tiny hamlet of Chop Gate in Bilsdale alone. I can well remember the local "lock up" just below the post office, where until a few years ago a signboard on the wall warned miners of the stern punishment meted out for riotous and disorderly behaviour. The miners were indeed a rough lot: they lived in their caves for weeks at a time and, like the gold prospectors of the Wild West, came down on monthly pay days to roister, fight and gamble their money away. Fives against a gable wall and quoits played on soft clay pitches were among the more respectable of their gambling habits.

The jet was worked in a somewhat elementary fashion. A narrow cave was excavated in the hillside or cliff and the shale brought out in a tub or wheelbarrow (see illustration on page 54). The fragments of jet were put on one side and the rubble simply tipped below the mouth of the cave. This explains the long rows of small waste heaps which stretch for mile after mile along the hillsides in Bilsdale, Raisdale and Scugdale.

Jet was reputed to have curative, even magical, properties. The caves at Runswick Bay are known as the Hob Holes, and the hob or fairy who haunted the holes was reputedly able to cure the whooping cough. It may well be that when the jet miners were active, the dust, particularly if it was burned with driftwood or seaweed, did have some effect on ailing lungs. The fame of our jet had reached beyond these shores. Marbodus of Rheims, *circa* 1430, wrote in his *Lapidarium* of its unique qualities and quite astonishing powers:

"The female womb its piercing fumes relieve,
  Nor falling sickness can this test deceive;
  It cures the dropsy, loosened teeth are fixed,
  Washed with the powdered stone in water mixed."

By contrast the alum industry was a complicated mining process which completely changed the shape of the highest cliffs and several of the most prominent crags overlooking the vale of the Tees. The alum shales were quarried in such vast quantities that the present contours of Kettleness, Rockcliff, Sandsend, Roseberry, Carlton Bank and Slape Wath bear little resemblance to their outlines on the prints of seventeenth-century lithographers. The smoke and stench of the alum workings were notorious—and with good reason: the process called for decaying seaweed boiled in urine, the latter commodity often having to be shipped from the metropolis itself. Alum was in urgent demand for dyes, tanning and medicinal purposes. Its value was known in the Middle Ages, but the Italians had the secret of its manufacture. It is easy therefore to accept the old story that Thomas Challoner kidnapped a couple of
workmen from the Papal works at Puteoli, and was duly

damned with bell, book and candle for his temerity. The truth, however, is far more humdrum. Like most "inventions", alum manufacture in Britain was not the result of a sudden Eureka-like inspiration. The process and the place were decided on only after more than a century of experiment and exploration, involving long and expensive litigation and even, at times, pure piracy. It is perhaps true that one of the Challoner family, having carried out experiments in Ireland, Flanders and the Midlands, eventually recognised the shales near Guisborough. The manufacture remained a monopoly of the early Stuart kings who were determined to avoid asking Parliament for money, but after the execution of Charles I in 1649, the Royalists lost their sole rights and the industry spread rapidly along the hills to the west and the cliffs to the east.

Every Teesside schoolboy knows the story of John Vaughan who, while walking on the Eston hills, struck his toe on a particularly heavy stone. Its weight and coloration convinced him that it was ironstone, and so, the apocryphal story goes, the Cleveland iron industry was born! As readers will have noted, there was an Iron Age in the Cleveland of the Ancient Britons, and the Rievaulx Estate was producing possibly as much as four hundred tons of high quality iron per annum until the Duke of Buckingham was dispossessed by Parliament during the Civil War.

The topmost seam of ironstone is found in the Eller Beck beds of the Middle Jurassic period, which were worked in medieval times at Botton Head, near the Cleveland Way, and the stone perhaps smelted in streamside bloomeries below Baysdale Abbey. The Romano-Britons around Hood Grange below Whitestone Cliff and the monks of Rievaulx used this inferior quality stone. The Pecten and Main seams are found in the Liassic rocks and were developed after many years of experiment along the coast where these old layers are exposed. From the middle of the eighteenth century ironstone had been collected from the shore and shipped to the Tyneside ironworks. If you are particularly observant or fortunate, you may see the foundations of the old wooden jetties under the cliffs at several points between Saltburn and Sandsend. Various amateur historians have assured me that they exist, and some of the published papers of local archaeological groups make reference to such structures, but I have not had the good fortune to see them for myself.

After some time local workmen began shovelling any sort of red heavy stone into their barrows and complaints of the quality of "sea-iron" became more frequent. In 1827 a certain Mr. Bewick came to investigate and from his observations of the strata exposed at Boulby concluded that rich seams of ironstone could be mined not only near the coast but on the slopes of the inland hills and dales. He urged Tyneside iron-masters to capitalise on his discoveries but it was twenty years before Cleveland's "Iron Rush" got under way. Bewick himself became manager of one of the earliest mines at Grosmont and John Vaughan bought ore from him and shipped it to Whitby to be smelted at Witton Park in the South Durham coalfield. Impressed by Bewick's story of a vast ironfield, Vaughan confidently opened up a mine at Eston and built six smelting furnaces close to the mines in 1852. Today not a single ironmine is working, but the pyramids of iron shale remain as landmarks all along the Cleveland Way from Roseberry Topping to Kettleness.

Jet jewellery

Helmsley to Sutton Bank

(about 7 miles including an extension of 2 miles to Roulston Scar and the White Horse)

The cross in the market square of Helmsley marks the beginning of the Cleveland Way and the first sector— from Helmsley to the edge of the escarpment of the Hambleton Hills—covers about seven miles. Starting from the cross, you follow the road to Stokesley (B1257) for a few yards, then turn off to the left along a signposted lane to Rievaulx. This is a recent diversion and some Ordnance maps show the old route via Griff Farm.

The older path left the lane and branched to the right; you now go straight ahead to the end of the lane and then, after two or three fields, turn down to the left, to the woodside. Avoid the field road which follows the wire through the fields. You are now walking along the edge of a wooded valley with, on the left, a crumbling wall. Most of the giant trees have been felled and the stumps give the impression of huge dining tables.

Two stiles give access to cultivated fields and then a new gate on the left takes you down into the valley. Cross the valley, following the track across the edge of Duncombe Park, and passing the site of the Polish Army camp on your left among the trees. You soon emerge into an open pasture, keeping a rather ornate little lodge on your right. Follow the edge of the steep valley for a few yards, then drop gently down to the motor road at Abbott Hag Wood above Rievaulx.

Follow the road for about a mile and a half, unless you wish to turn right at the bridge to see the abbey. Note the Wombwell coat of arms on the cottage by the bridge, and its garden, in spring and summer, ablaze with flowers.

The road swings up one of the dry valleys to the south towards Scawton, but you must follow the track parallel 59

E

White Horse, Kilburn

to the stream—a forestry road which is now metalled.
It makes a wide sweep at the foot of the next valley in
order to avoid a broad stream which comes bubbling
out of the roots of a tree (the presence of a spring makes
it a delightful spot for a picnic lunch). To avoid this
detour you have the choice of a short-cut—over a small
plank bridge and through a gated path in the thicket.

Continuing along the forestry track to the next dry
valley, which is Flassen Dale, you turn up this broad
dale for a few yards only, then go up a narrow overgrown gully which you should find signposted. This
sunken way brings you out into Low Field Lane, leading into Cold Kirby. At the west end of the village a
walled lane leads off to the left. At the end of the lane
the Cleveland Way is routed diagonally across the
60 fields to the racing stables of Hambleton House. A

metalled road runs from Hambleton House to the A170 which you strike near the Hambleton Hotel. Opposite the hotel a drive takes you through the plantation to the edge of the escarpment. At this point you may proceed south along the edge for about a mile and a half for the view from Roulston Scar and the land above the White Horse, but you will have to retrace your steps. The main path turns north to reach the car park at Sutton Bank, the terminus of our first stage.

There are only one or two places where anyone walking in the opposite direction needs to exercise caution. It may be better to take the ride on the south side of the fields of Hambleton House and join the lane to Kirby by the overgrown field road at the end of the first large field rather than go through the stable yard and diagonally across the walled pastures.

On leaving Cold Kirby in the marshy valley below the church, do not be tempted to take the gated road down the valley but turn up to the right to the road along the ridge.

Soon after turning off the road beyond Rievaulx, you climb up through Whinny Bank Wood. At the top are two gates; take the one on the left into the fields; the other road follows the escarpment for a quarter mile or so to the park round Duncombe Hall, a showpiece designed by Vanburgh in the style of Castle Howard and Blenheim, but unfortunately not on the Cleveland Way.

Dark green fritillary butterfly

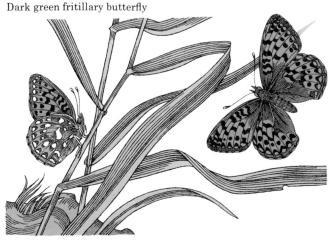

Maps reference

Class 1 Road	A170
„ 2 „	Fenced B1262 Unfenced
Roads Under Construction	
Other Roads	Good, metalled Poor, or unmetalled
Footpaths	*FP* *FP* Fenced Unfenced
Railways, Multiple Track	Station Road over *FB* Sidings Cutting Tunnel (Footbridge)
„ Single Track	Level Crossing Embankment Viaduct Road under
„ Narrow Gauge	
Aerial Ropeway	*Aerial Ropeway*
Boundaries County or County Borough	
„ „ „ „ „ with Parish	
„ Parish	
Pipe Line (Oil, Water)	Pipe Line
Electricity Transmission Lines (Pylons shown at bends and spaced conventionally)	

Post Offices (in Villages & Rural Areas only) ......**P** Town Hall ......**TH** Public House ......***PH***

Church or Chapel with Tower ......▮ Church or Chapel with Spire ......▮ Church or Chapel without either ......+

Triangulation Station ......△ on Church with Tower ......⨹ without Tower ......⨺

Intersected Point on Chy ......○ on Church with Spire ......⨀ without Spire ......+ on Building ......▭

Guide Post ......***GP.*** Mile Post ......***MP.*** Mile Stone ......***MS.*** Boundary Stone ......***BS*** ○ Boundary Post ......***BP***○

Youth Hostel ......**Y** Telephone Call Box (Public) ......**T** *(AA)* **A** (RAC) **R** Antiquity (site of) ......✛

Public Buildings	▬
Quarry & Gravel Pit	
National Trust Area	Scarth Wood Moor NT
Osier Bed	
Reeds	
Park, Fenced	
Wood, Coniferous, Fenced	
Wood, Non-Coniferous Unfenced	
Brushwood, Fenced & Unfenced	

Glasshouses	
Orchard	
Furze	
Rough Pasture Heath & Moor	
Marsh	
Well	*W* ○
Spring	*Spr* ○
Wind Pump	***Wd Pp.***

Entry Cleveland Way

Contours are at 25 feet vertical interval, shown broken in built up areas.

Spot Height ......*123*·

Ferries Sand Hills
Foot Vehicle *HWMMT* Mud Flat Rock
Slopes
HWMMT △ Beacon Sand
Lake Highest point to which ⚓ Lightship
Bridge Medium Tides flow
Canal Lock Weir Sand & Shingle
Towing Aqueduct Ford FB Cliff
Path (Footbridge) Lighthouse

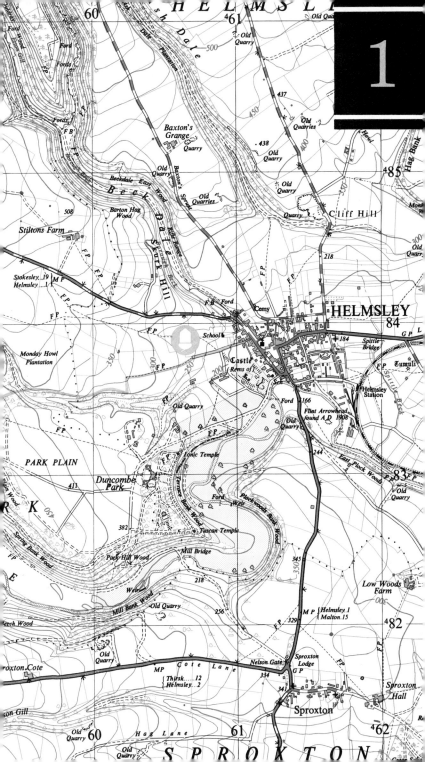

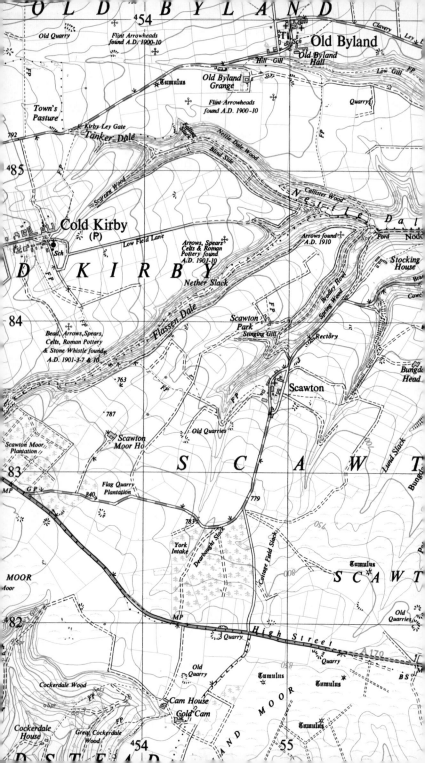

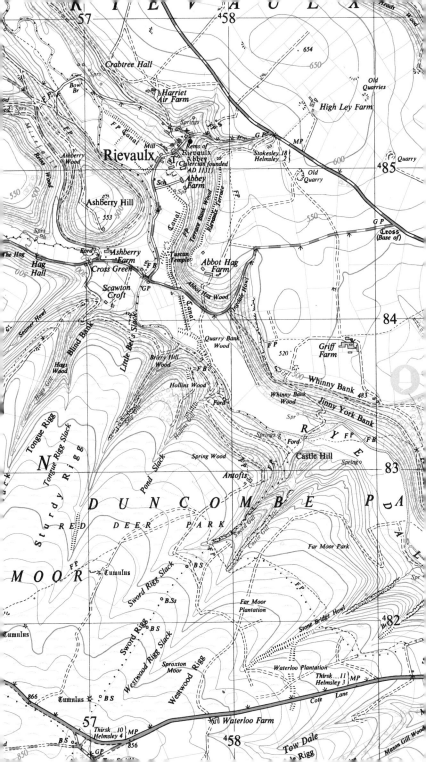

Sutton Bank to Osmotherley

(13-14 miles)

Route-finding from White Mare Crag near Sutton Bank Top to Osmotherley is fairly easy; so are the walking conditions through short grass and some bracken, gorse and heather.

The Way, at first, is unmistakable: no forks to right or left until a path is reached leading down to Gormire —part of the Gormire nature trail. Farther on, one or two fairly well-worn paths in the grass above the wide curved basin of the South Woods need cause little trouble as they run more or less parallel with the Way.

The Way now starts to climb over rougher ground and I have known walkers to take a rather obvious track below Boltby Scar, partly because one or two old walls and frail wire fences seem to block the right of way up to the site of the old fort on top of the scar. Keep above the scar and the huge quarries on the left, however, and with field walls on your right make for High Barn, a farmhouse half-hidden by a prominent screen of trees. Pass this farmhouse on your right. Beyond the farm the Way is criss-crossed by animal and cart tracks, but as the Romans said: *Tutissime in medio ibis*—"thou shalt go most safely in the middle"—veer neither to your right through the wall, nor steeply down to your left.

The Way in fact goes more or less right across the middle of the field, to a gate in the north wall giving access to the lane, known as Sneck Yate, above Boltby village. Cross straight over the lane to enter a young plantation and follow the narrow, flower-decked path through the trees—in spring, summer and even into November you will find colour here. The path emerges into rough scrubland with the homestead of Low Paradise just ahead.

67

Black Hambleton

A white road climbs up to High Paradise, which is kept on your right as you circle the farm to reach the Hambleton Drove Road via a large gate in the northeast corner of a broad pasture field beyond the farmhouse. All is now straightforward, in every sense of the word, for some four miles, the trees of Boltby forest affording pleasant shelter for part of the way. You reach the walled enclosures of the drovers' hostelry—Limekiln House—now in ruins. There must have been a good water supply here and the walls still offer shelter to rest and eat but, despite the presence of tall reeds, I have never located a spring.

A mile beyond Limekiln House careless walkers have been known to follow the obvious path straight ahead over Black Hambleton and have landed down in
68 Snilesworth. The Way, however, turns left along the

wallside: there is a Moors Path sign but it was pointing vaguely skywards the last time I passed it. After another couple of miles the road becomes very rough and deeply sunken as it drops down the shoulder of Black Hambleton, and the footsore will find some ease in walking on the turf and heather on the left of the road—we call it the "cam" in this part of the world.

Soon after reaching the level moor, the Drove Road joins up with the motor road from Helmsley. Here the Way turns down through the bracken into Oak Dale, although if you are in a hurry you can follow the road into Osmotherley. There is, as yet, no beaten path down into Oak Dale, but provided you make for the wall seen above the north side of the reservoir and keep the Oakdale Beck well below you on your left you should avoid trouble.

Above: Cote Garth Mill, near Osmotherley

Top left: Oakdale reservoir

Bottom left: Osmotherley. Way continues through passageway (left) between houses

As the map shows, you have to cross a little gill running down to the reservoir from the north. The crossing is made just at the north-east corner of the wood which screens the reservoir. You then follow the wallside on your left to a stone-stepped stile a hundred yards beyond the stream. Keeping fairly close to the water's edge, and then over a couple of pastures, brings you to a cart bridge below the deserted Oak Dale Farm. A good farm road leads to the motor road which you cross to enter Green Lane below Rose Cottage.

At the top of a rise in the lane, turn left towards

White House Farm and continue almost straight down the hill to a footbridge in the wood, climb a stepped path and cross the middle of the pastures towards the tower of Osmotherley Church.

There are only two or three places to be wary of if you are walking in the reverse direction. You start from Osmotherley through a narrow covered way on the east side of the war memorial in the square.

Look out for the stone stile in the wall at the east end of the reservoir in Oak Dale. Cross Jenny Brewster's Gill—do not follow the worn path alongside it. Black Hambleton is an unmistakable landmark and the scar of the sunken road is clearly visible.

There should be no difficulty in finding the entry to High Paradise pasture as it is the only building for miles around. There is also a Moors Path signpost.

Beyond High Paradise it is tempting to keep going down the road but you must keep above Low Paradise, take the narrow path through the forest and cross straight over Sneck Yate Lane to High Barn.

Peacock butterfly

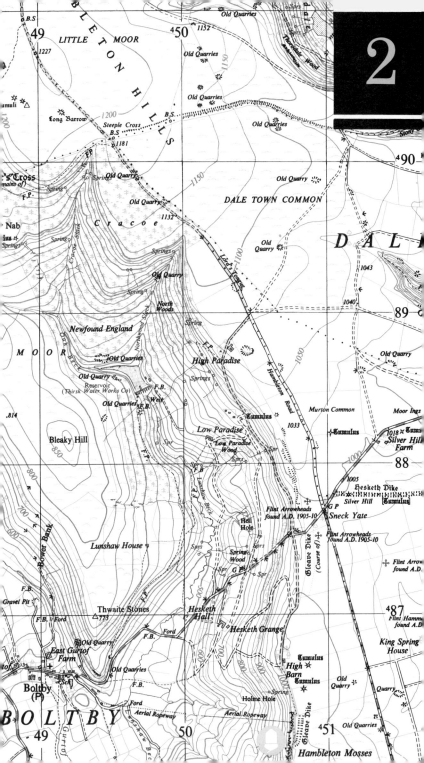

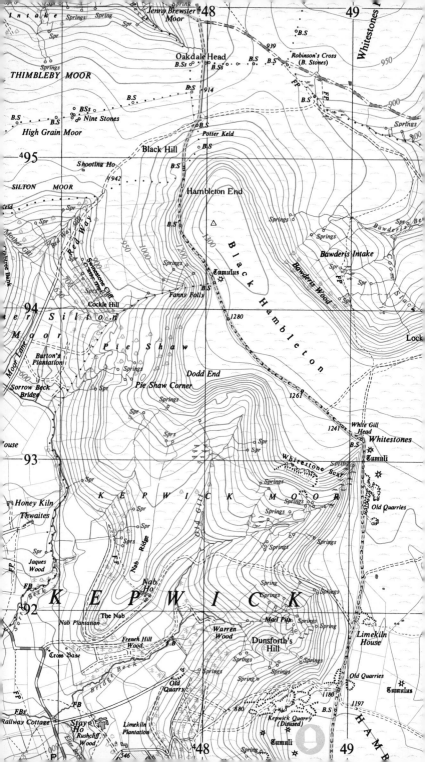

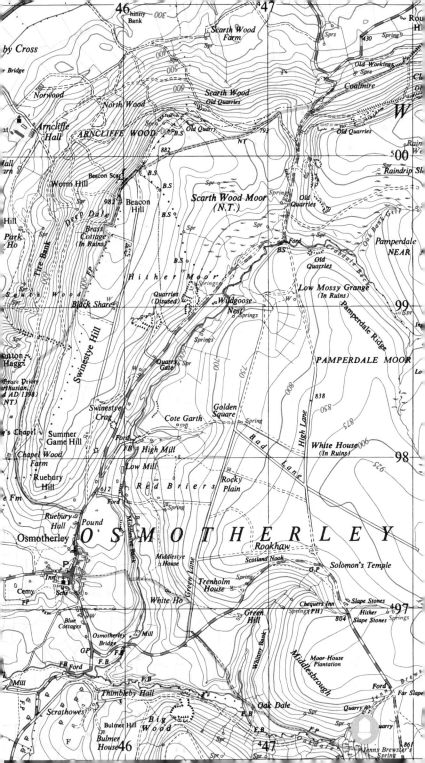

Osmotherley to Kildale

(18–19 miles)

As most of this stretch follows the signposted Lyke
Wake Walk, comparatively little direction is needed.
From Osmotherley market cross you take the road
north towards Swainby. At the top of the village street
a lane runs off to the left. If the vandals have not struck,
there should be two signposts—the usual carved Moors
Path sign and a white finger post indicating the way to
the Lady Catherine Chapel.

This lane takes you round the shoulder of Ruebury
Hill: in a short while it forks; you take the lower path
on the left to pass Chapel Wood Farm, and then go
straight ahead along the wallside for three fields.
Beyond the fields you enter a plantation and fork
sharply up to the right to the G.P.O. beacons, site of
the former Brass Cottage. The left fork from the fields
would take you down to Mount Grace Priory, from
where a forestry road leads along the foot of the hills to
Arncliffe Hall. You could then rejoin the Way by a
path from the hall to Scarth Nick. Keep the wall on
your right from the G.P.O. beacons to the concrete
triangulation point on the other side of the wall, which
marks the start of the Lyke Wake Walk.

As you drop down the open moor to Scarth Nick you
see far ahead the well-trodden path which descends the
north face of Coalmire. There is a chance of going
wrong here. At the foot of Coalmire you must keep to
the red shale road well above the stream even though
O.S. maps show a right of way closer to the banks of
Scugdale Beck. You keep to this road up Scugdale for
about a mile. The overgrown ground on the left provides
good cover for pheasants.

When you come abreast of Hollin Hill, seen on the
76 north side of Scugdale, you turn steeply down a pasture

Mount Grace Priory

and cross the beck near its confluence with a tributary stream. At this point you join a rough road coming down from Harfa Bank Farm, passing Hollin Hill Farm on your left. This field road takes you up to the hamlet of Huthwaite Green, where a well-used track leads through old mine workings up to the forest and then, turning left, runs north-east along the forestry fence.

The path turns sharply up to Live Moor; by now it is an enclosed track which can be extremely slippery in wet weather. At the end of the track, swing half-right. The Way over the moor is fairly well hollowed out and clearly defined. In fact it continues like this for some miles. In wet weather it becomes more like a stream, causing one wag to enquire if Bill Cowley, the founder of the Lyke Wake Walk, was offering a prize to anyone completing the route by canoe!

If you are out on the moor in blustery weather or a gale force wind, you would do well to use the sheltered jet miners' trod which runs alongside the forestry wall well below the high peaks all the way to Carlton Bank and Hasty Bank.

A few walkers have been misled when crossing the gap between Cringle Moor and Cold Moor and indeed a

Scarth Nick, looking over Coalmire with Roseberry Topping in the far distance

track has been worn over the walled pasture by folk who have missed the correct route. Instead of climbing the wall, you work your way round to the north and take a gate into the field. Then, turn up to your left, passing close to the Wain Stones, to continue due east over the crest of Hasty Bank. Signs help to keep you on the Lyke Wake Walk track, down an enclosed path and across the main Stokesley-Helmsley road. You go through the gate on the south side of the forestry boundary wall and climb straight up to the sunken path through the crags.

The well-worn track of the Lyke Wake Walk takes you in a gentle curve over Botton Head, the highest point (1,489 feet) of the Cleveland Hills. A triangulation point on the remains of a huge stone burial mound attests this fact, and it was from here probably that William the Conqueror saw the smoke from the fires in

York. The howe marks the northern end of the Danish-named track—Thurkilsty—which linked York and Cleveland.

You walk for about twenty minutes along the broad fire break to the east of Round Hill on Botton Head, then the Way swings south-east to where the narrow road along Rudland Rigg crossed the Rosedale Railway at Bloworth Crossing. There is also a short-cut to the Rudland Rigg road by a second fire break which runs north-east. This patch of moor used to be extremely boggy before drainage ditches were dug. It is worth taking this short-cut which goes through an old railway cutting. Beyond the cutting, due north-east, you cross rough grassland to reach the Rudland Rigg road near an old cross which marks the parish boundaries.

You now have a four- to five-mile tramp along rough moor road. You leave the Ingleby Greenhow road just 79

Above: View from Cringle Moor, showing the Cleveland escarpment

Left: Carlton village

beyond a stone signpost on the left and turn north-east across the open moor at a closed gate—strangely enough there is no fence to go with the gate, it has obviously been put there to deter motorists. This road is quite recent, the older heather-covered sunken ways can be traced alongside. You strike the tarmac road which comes up from Baysdale Abbey on your right. Join this road and continue straight ahead for a mile, then turn down through the Park Dyke and follow the road into Kildale village.

For those walking from Kildale westwards, the route is even easier to follow. One or two places demand a little attention.

Avoid turning left a mile or so beyond Park Dyke when the tarmac road swings down into Baysdale. Between Cold Moor and Cringle Moor, remember to cross to the north boundary wall of the enclosed field and make your way round it.

When you have turned along the narrow road opposite the telephone kiosk at Huthwaite Green, be sure to swing down to your right beyond the footbridge and concrete bridge over Scugdale Beck. Then just beyond the bridge, make your way from the second little stream almost straight up the pasture; there is, as yet, no worn path but the grass on the Way is short and smooth. Thistles thrive on either side—it is obvious why.

Male merlin with young

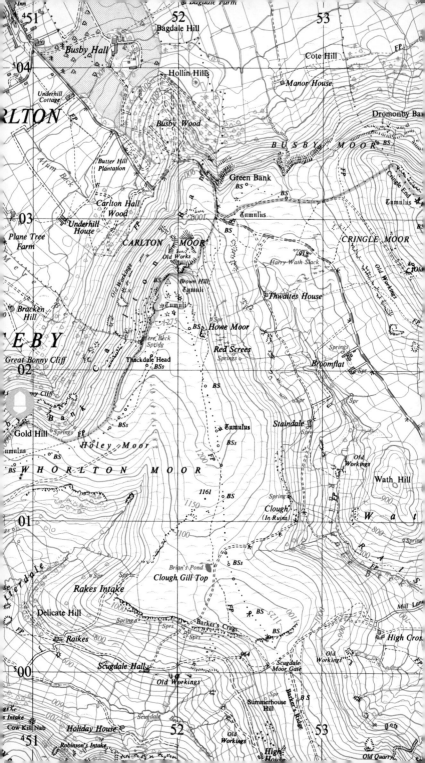

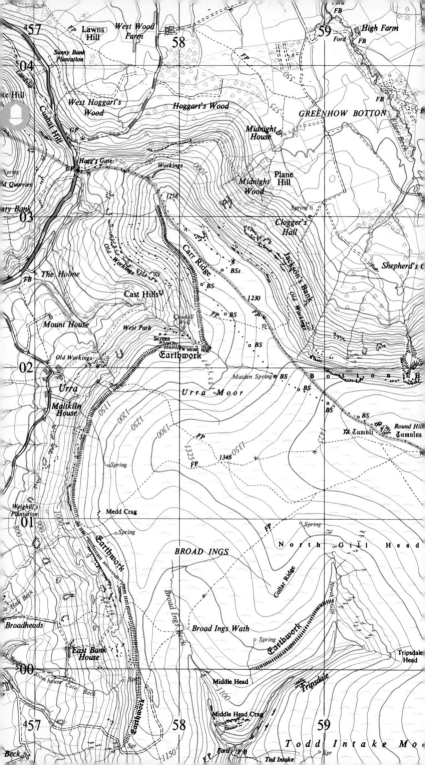

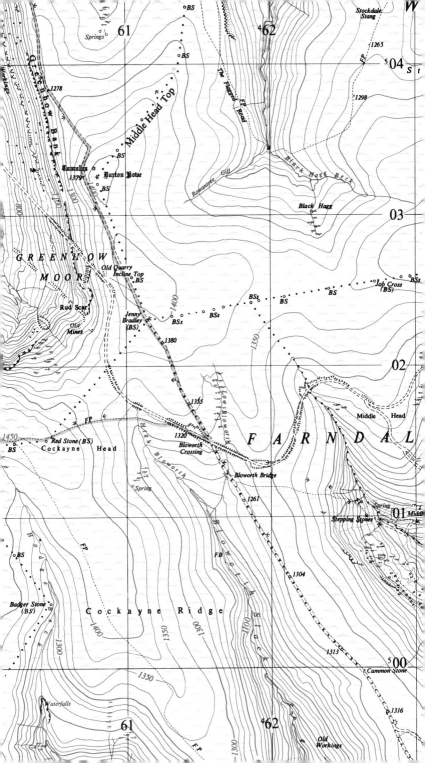

Kildale to Saltburn

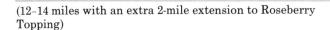

(12-14 miles with an extra 2-mile extension to Roseberry Topping)

At the bottom of the hill below Kildale post office (ice cream and minerals on sale), turn left and take the first turn right—a gated road—to Guisborough. From the old pine trees at the top of the hill above Bankside Farm, a broad forestry walk takes you almost due west to Captain Cook's monument, where you turn north and drop down to the car park at Gribdale Gate.

The Way now hugs the wall on the west side of Great Ayton Moor for almost two and a half miles. At a corner where two walls meet is a bridle gate; enthusiasts will cross the gap to climb Roseberry Topping, returning the same way. The next stage of the Way is quite clear for half a mile across the open moor up towards a standing stone, which unfortunately has a drunkard's habit of falling down.

There is, as yet, no clear track over the crest of the hill, and most walkers go down to a forestry ride rather too far to the north of the line of the right of way marked on the map. However, if the day is clear, you cannot miss your objective—the great crag of Highcliff with a roll collar of old oak trees behind its dome. You must first cross the rough moorland road coming up from Hutton Lowcross. If you are walking early in the year before the bracken is high you can easily pick out the sunken track marking the way to the enclosed fields round Codhill Farm, but in summer bracken hides the Way and it is advisable to use a sheep track through the heather.

Eventually you drop down into Codhill, and be careful to hug the wall on your left, as in a wet summer this broad valley, the shallows of an Ice Age lake, reverts to a vast marsh.

You must climb up the south shoulder of Highcliff 89

Roseberry Topping in close-up

and make your way close to the edge of the cliffs for a few hundred yards. Beyond Highcliff, forestry rides offer a bewildering choice of route for the next mile or two. The local Ramblers' Association has marked boulders and posts with the white acorn sign but these are not always permitted to remain *in situ* for very long. The best advice I can give is to keep fairly well up towards the top of the ridge. At its eastern end is a bridle path, just over the drainage ditch on your right, leading into a rough pasture. You continue almost north-east across a stony gully under some dwarf trees to a second gate where you strike a rough field road from Round Close Farm. Drop down this road and look out for a narrow path between a hedge and a concrete and wire fence on the right. It ends in an overgrown path through self-sown alder and hazel bushes. According to

your map, this path should take you to the village of

Charlton Terrace. Unfortunately the huge tips of alum shale hereabouts are being extensively quarried and the delineation of the Way tends to suffer—a temporary inconvenience, it is hoped.

You cannot fail to see the "Fox and Hounds" inn which marks the spot where Wayfarers must cross the main road.

When you reach the woodside above the quarry on the north side of the road, the path soon merges into a field road which becomes more and more distinct as you draw near to Airy Hill Farm. Beyond this the Way is well metalled into Skelton.

There are many possible ways of negotiating the various groups of houses, but once in the main street you must leave the township for the Riftswood path along Derwentwater Road near the public library and police station. A gate leads into the fields and the 91

Highcliff from Roseberry Common

path is signposted. The path is very well trodden over the corn and pasture fields into the wood: there is a broad roundabout path and a much steeper direct path to the footbridge directly under the tall arches of the railway viaduct. The Way then continues alongside the old mill race, but when you come into sight of the former Marske Mill, you turn sharply up to the left along a cobbled pack-horse lane which reaches Saltburn not far from the Youth Hostel.

If you are not staying at the Hostel, keep to the path which leaves the narrow lane on the right. This runs north above the stream through the woods and ornamental gardens to the shore at Old Saltburn.

Adder

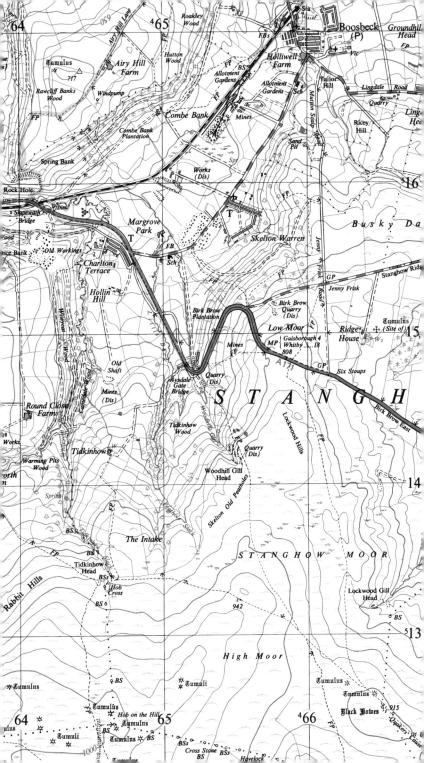

Saltburn to Whitby

(19 miles)

From Old Saltburn the Cleveland Way climbs to the top of Hunt Cliff. According to the map, the path should leave the beach a few yards beyond the "Old Ship Inn". It is advisable, however, in wet weather to take the narrow track behind the inn, which leads to the coast-guard cottages and follows a well-defined track to join the cliff edge path.

While you are within the boundaries of the Saltburn Urban District Council there is no protecting fence along the cliff edge; as soon as you enter the Skelton and Brotton U.D.C. there is protection on the seaward side. Even so, continual cliff falls are to be expected and fence posts will occasionally have disappeared into the sea.

As you round the highest point of Hunt Cliff, walking on the cinder bed of the railway track for a short distance, you have, on your left, what is perhaps the most awesome view of any part of the Way, the cliff facing almost directly northwards into the full flow of tide, current and swell.

Beyond the highest point, the path runs at some distance from the cliff edge alongside pasture and arable fields to the slag tips at Skinningrove Steel Works. It is almost impossible to get down the sheer cliffs of slippery boulder clay at any point until you reach the narrow valley into which the slag has been tipped. You must make your way down the edge of the slag to the beach. Not so long ago the track ran along a sharp ridge of boulder clay (still to be seen on your left), but the path has become more perilous every year. In the spring of 1970 the slag was very rough indeed, more daunting than the Lake District's famous Wast- 97

From Boulby, looking to Hinderwell and Staithes

water Screes, but time and strong boots have reduced the rigours of the descent, and complaints are less frequent.

You make your way along the beach and cross the end of the old jetty close to the pumping station to reach Skinningrove village. Cross the rust-coloured stream and follow the tarmac road that first runs seawards and then turns back to climb the cliff.

Some walkers scramble directly up the cliff along the side of the fence but the line of the Way, and the safer approach, starts by using the road. Towards the top of the first steep pitch, a stile on the left leads into a rough pasture; go straight across to the cliff edge path which continues on the seaward side of the field fences to Warsett Hill above Hummersea Bay.

Keeping fairly close to the cliff edge, you reach two
fenced-in ponds, their water discoloured by waste

effluents. You then take an obvious and direct route by a field road through the tiny farmstead of Warren House, two fields beyond the ponds.

Keep on the seaward side of the field walls and fences until you come to the pastures above Boulby village, where you turn sharply down along the wallside. The route down to the retired miners' cottages at Cowbar is clearly seen from the cliff top.

A short stretch of road takes you through Cowbar, down to Staithes and along the harbour wall to the east end, you climb up Church Street along a narrow gully, passing St. Peter's Church. Just above the church another gully forks off to the left and a well trodden path takes you over the hill to Port Mulgrave. The grass is high on the cliff top—if there has been rain or heavy dew, you will be drenched to the armpits.

Be careful as you approach Runswick Bay from Port

Mulgrave. You must leave the cliff edge and turn sharply to the right along a hedge: a tiny pond half-hidden among iris flags and tall reeds marks this turning point to the top of Runswick village.

You follow the beach as far as the narrow valley running up from Hob Holes to Claymoor. The aptness of the name becomes only too obvious in wet weather when the greasy grey-brown surface puts a premium on firm footholding so that going up or down is a hazard, especially for elderly walkers whose balance and reflexes may no longer be what they once were.

There is an alternative route by public path from the beach huts at Runswick, via Northfields, Westfields and Barnby Tofts, which rejoins the Claymoor to Kettleness path, but involving about two miles of additional walking.

The Cleveland Way crosses the steep gully of Catbeck on the east side of the blue and white bungalow. Beyond Kettleness, a double track leads to the coast-guard look-out. The path follows the cliff edge and seemingly peters out in some high scrub and briar. You must climb up over the embankment of the old railway and resume your way eastwards along the edge of the pasture fields, with the hedge and fence on your left.

You will have to keep a sharp look-out for the steep steps leading through the hawthorn bushes down to the old railway track in the gully of Overdale. Follow the track into Sandsend.

There is a long trudge up the main Whitby road to the golf course where you can turn off to the left on to the cliff edge path to Whitby Spa, but the beach is always a preferable alternative when the tide permits.

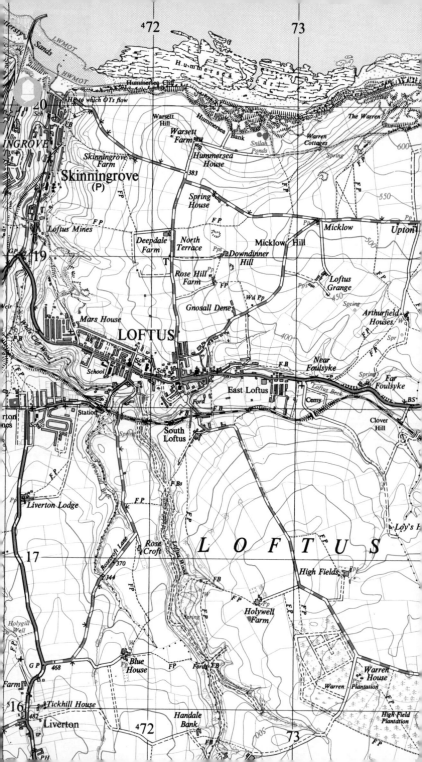

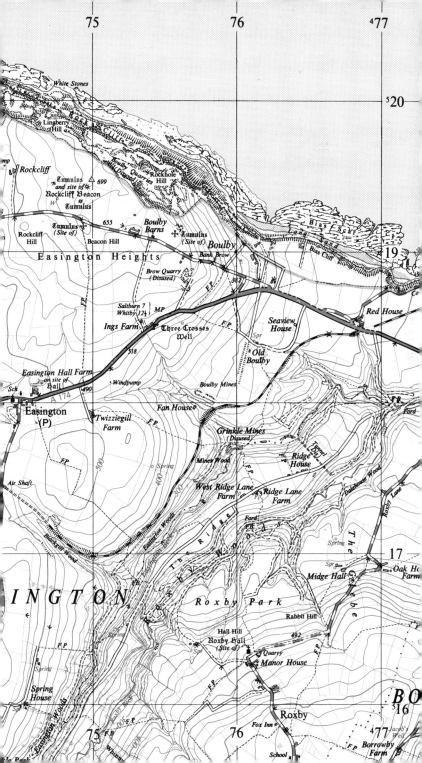

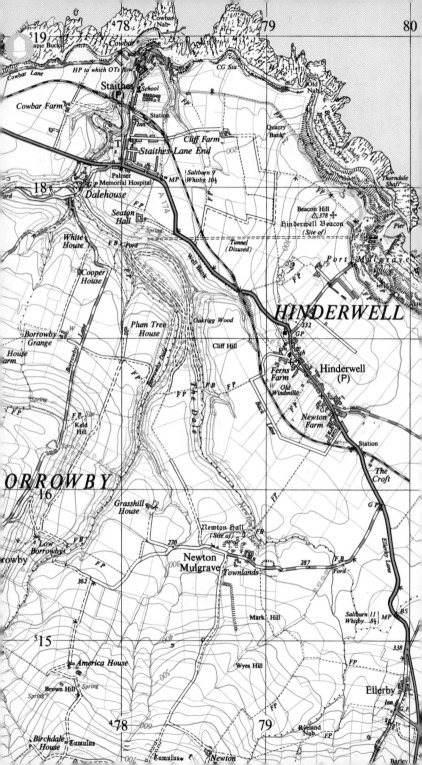

81 82 ⁴83 ⁵19

18

17

Lingrow Knock

Howe
arrow

Wrack Hill

Quarry
End

Lingrow End
Topman
End

Firs

Runswick
Bank Top

Runswick
(P)

Dabdlike Stones

Great Ship

Jarvis' Landing
Hole

Caldron

RUNSWICK BAY

16

Kettleness
Scar

Barton
Kettle Ness
Wind Hole

ttle Dale
End

Ing
End

Dother Pits

Nettlea

Stones
Catbeck Trod
Catbeck Hill

HWMOT Kettleness

Hill

Old Iron Workings
Coastguard
Sta

Cliff

Dunsley
Dale End

Dunsley Dale

Limekiln Beck

Hob Holes

Redscar Hole

White Stones

Old Mine

Kettlene

Sunny Bank

Bornby Dales

Randy Bell

Randy Bell
End

Ford
Claymoor
End

High Cliff

Cliff

Whitestones

FP

Cawl

ROM

.369

FP

Mines
(Dis)

Old
Shaft

Butter Howe

FP

15

se

Coverdale Lane

FB

Northfields
Farm

81

Iron
House

FB

Claymoor

Wilsey Toft

Dismantled Railway

82

FP

Platymill

FP

Brockrigg

B r o c k r i g g

FP

Cow Hill

Tumulus

⁴83

Tumulus

Tumulus

Stone

Slangoe
Cart

Whinny
Hill

Spr

300

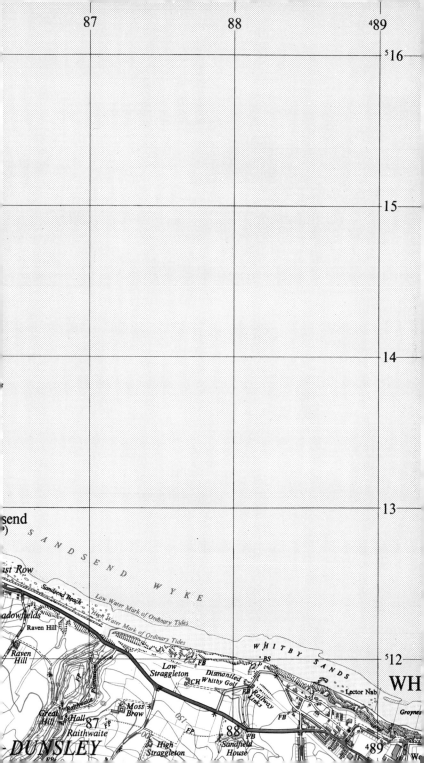

87　　　　　　88　　　　⁴89

⁵16

15

14

13

send
⁵)

S A N D S E N D　　*W Y K E*

ust Row

Sandsend Beach

Low Water Mark of Ordinary Tides

adowfields

High Water Mark of Ordinary Tides

Raven Hill

W H I T B Y　*S A N D S*

BS

Raven
Hill

Low
Straggleton
CH

Dismantled
Whitby Golf

FB

FB
⁵12

Railway
Links

WH

FB

Lector Nab

Great
Hill
Hall

Raithwaite
Plantation

Moss
Brow

FB

Groynes

87　FP
Raithwaite

High
Straggleton

88

FB

Sandfield
House

⁴89

DUNSLEY

We

Whitby to Scarborough

(19 miles)

You start the cliff walk from Whitby to Scarborough by a gate at the roadside at Abbey Farm. The path is more than well used by thousands of holidaymakers passing between the Saltwick Bay caravan sites and the town. From the coastguard look-out post close to Abbey Farm, the path runs fairly close along the cliff edge for half a mile, finally turning inland through the main walk (or drive) of the caravan and camping site of Saltwick Bay. You turn back towards the cliff edge once more on the south side of Saltwick Bay, and the path to the two large coastguard stations, less than a mile beyond Saltwick Bay, is well trodden.

Hereabouts walkers have gone astray. The path runs outside the first group of buildings. A stile over a broken wall beyond the first building leads into a pasture, as you keep the second building on your left. A large white notice board stands out against the gorse bushes on the hillside, but not until you are close to it do you see the double Coast Path sign. Here you turn left along a level path which has been cut in the turf beyond the fog signal building. You make your way up towards a white fingerpost at the side of a stile at the edge of Beacon Hill.

The route presents no real difficulties as far as Robin Hood's Bay, except for two steep gullies which can be tricky in wet weather. On the other hand in dry and windy conditions on this stretch, the shale dust is whipped up in clouds.

You are now faced with some rather inconvenient stiles and one or two wicket gates which are difficult to negotiate with a large frame rucksack.

Nearly all the Youth Hostellers I have spoken with

Robin Hood's Bay

prefer to make their way between Boggle Hole and
Robin Hood's Bay by way of the shore. The official path,
of course, runs along the cliff top and a signpost opposite
the Bay Hotel in the town indicates a steep narrow
alleyway up to the cliffs.

After walking along the seaward side of three fields,
you come to The Nab above Boggle Hole Hostel. The
drop down between jutting stumps of old thornbushes
calls for considerable care: you really must look where
you are putting your feet. The steep road climbing the
south bank of the Hole might appear to be the Way, but
no, you go up a very narrow path leading off the road.
Once on the top you are again overlooking the sea but
after a few fields another difficult descent brings you
down into the Stoupe.

From here you do have to follow the road for about
a quarter mile beyond the farm at the top of the bank,

where an enclosed path on the left takes you to the cliff edge once again. You can see the Ravenscar Hotel perched on the high cliff—if it is not shrouded in a Cleveland "roak"—so you can hardly get lost.

But you may easily miss the designated track: in fact it seems that very few walkers do keep to the official right of way in the fields immediately below Browside Farm. There is a fairly well used path from the cliff edge diagonally across open pasture, but the Way is in fact signposted and takes a couple of sharply angled turns along the edge of the pastures, following a high fence and hedge. It rather looks as if there was an enclosed stone causeway here at one time, possibly used by pack-ponies from the alum works. You will note the large stone slab crossing over the shallow drainage channels.

You soon join the road from Browside Farm to 111

Ravenscar and find yourself on a shale road between bramble and gorse bushes. If you continue too far on this track, you swing round in a half-circle to Raven Hall Hotel golf course, only to find you have erred! The Way has recently been modified; you should leave the shale road for a narrow path on the right opposite one of the marker posts of the nature trail, climbing up through a wood to join a road below the old railway embankment which takes you to the café near the bus stop at Ravenscar village.

You take the station road running alongside the hotel grounds for a very short distance, then turn left across the fields to start the cliff edge walk again. You can save time by going up the old station road for about a mile, it is never more than a field away from the coast. Rather less than two miles south of Ravenscar, you will see a deserted look-out hut, convenient for a picnic break or shelter in a sudden squall.

The path alternates on the east and west of the field fence, winding its way occasionally under a thick canopy of blackthorn hedge. At least two rather alarming gaps in the path threaten the unwary with a hurried descent to the shore. You will be thankful for boots with a good tread.

Soon you are overlooking the tree-shrouded cliffs of Hayburn Wyke, dropping gently down to a steep path in which local scouts have cut steps and provided wooden treads. Rain has caused the heavy boulder clay to slide down, carrying away part of the path. Up or down—this is a real scramble and in wet weather everyone will get dirty.

At Hayburn Wyke, close to the shore, a footbridge crosses the stream and the path turns up the valley. After a short distance, the Way turns sharply up to the left, climbing steeply up through the bushes to resume its course along the cliffs. A screen of blackthorn on the seaward side provides welcome security when a north-east gale is blowing but otherwise spoils the view.

Cloughton Wyke, round which the Way swings in a half-circle, must impress you with its elaborate display of well-bedded brown sandstones interspersed with

Cove at Boggle Hole, Robin Hood's Bay

Waterfall on beach at Hayburn Wyke

blue-grey clays and silts which make the bay so attractive to geologists and photographers. The anglers on the rocky platforms below the east cliffs always seem to be hauling in their long lines heavy with catch, especially in the mackerel season.

It is useful to know that a road from Cloughton reaches the cliff edge at this point, and if tired or overdue at your destination, you can get a bus from Cloughton village. Support parties in cars can arrange to meet walkers at this point; after all Whitby to Scarborough

can be a long stretch for anyone out of training.

From Hundale it is all gentle downhill walking to Scalby Beck and the Scarborough north shore, and all the time the castle on its limestone crag is clearly in view. Those bound for the Scarborough Youth Hostel may avail themselves of a path just one field beyond Scalby Lodge, to be clearly seen from the cliff path. This avoids a long drop into the Scalby mills valley and climb back up to the hostel.

For trekkers from the south to the north-west, there 115

are only two places which present any difficulty, and one I have already mentioned—the crossing of Hayburn Wyke. The second comes just above the lighthouse at Saltwick. Walkers may tend to keep to an obvious path and field road well away from the cliff instead of dropping down to the coastguard stations between which the Way runs.

Whitby harbour and East Cliff (local lobster pots in foreground)

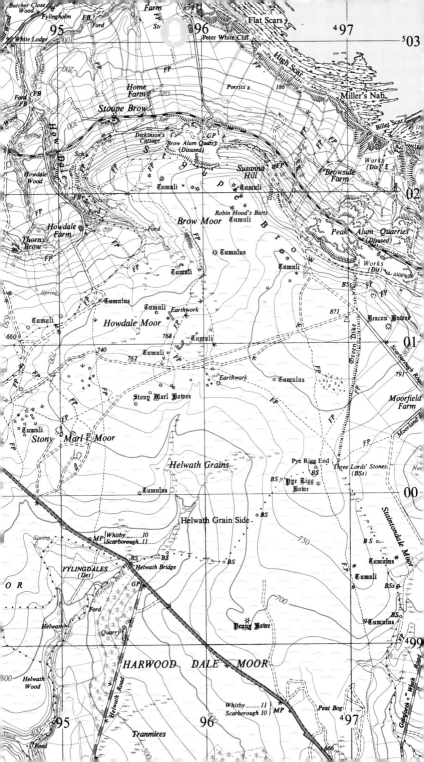

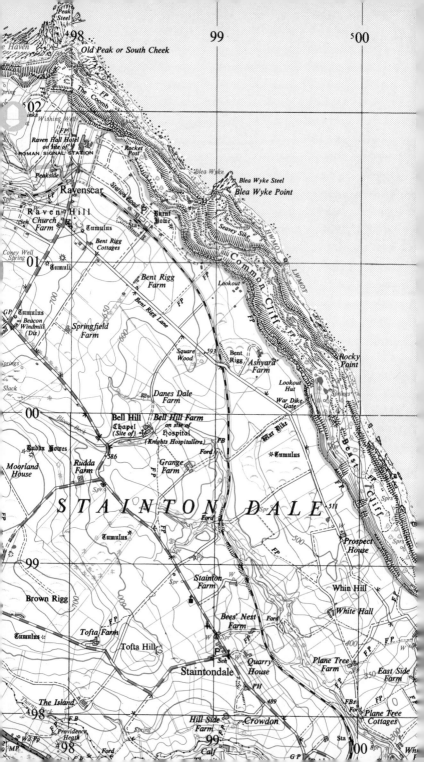

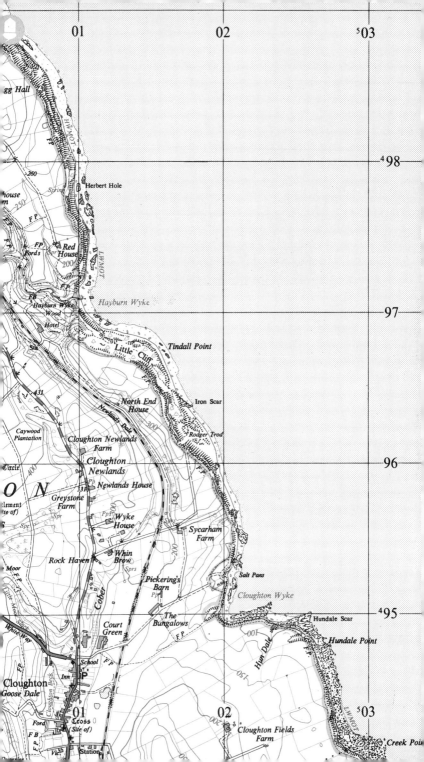

Scarborough to Filey

(7 miles)

Scarborough Castle (12th century)

Filey Brigg

The final section of the Way, from the ancient town of Scarborough to Filey Brigg, starts with two or three miles of highly urbanised paths, taking in promenades, shopping centres, amusement arcades—the usual paraphernalia of modern urban living—and leaving you finally above the Spa Gardens and below the South Cliff golf course. Alternatively, you can take a bus to Wheatcroft and drop down the fields, near the waterworks, to Cayton Bay.

If you walk along Scarborough's south cliff, you have to come up to the main Scarborough–Filey road (A165) at Osgodby Point by an enclosed path behind the NALGO holiday camp at Cayton Bay. You follow the

old road down to a stile on the left, leading into the fields and down to the cliff path, past a line of scattered bungalows which overlook Cayton Bay sands. This takes you to Red Cliff, a climb of just over two hundred feet.

You drop down again to Gristhorpe Bay and the chalets and bungalows, but the rocks of the Great Dike provide a pleasant contrast. Beyond the curved bay of the Wyke, you leave the holiday camps for a mile or two of good short-grassed walking on the clay cliffs of Newbiggin before reaching the north promenade at Filey.

The only difficult section for those travelling the

reverse direction occurs at Cayton Bay where you might be inclined to join the main road in the little gully at the lowest point of the cliffs. Instead, you cross the gully and make your way up above the water-works to the bend in the main road at the top of the hill. Follow the road for half a mile and keep a sharp look-out for the narrow path running alongside the holiday camp down to the screen of bushes on the cliff edge.

At low tide it is possible to avoid the road between Wheatcroft and Cayton by keeping to the beach and climbing Osgodby Point on the east side of the holiday camp. You rejoin the Way in the woods at the top of the cliffs.

Broom

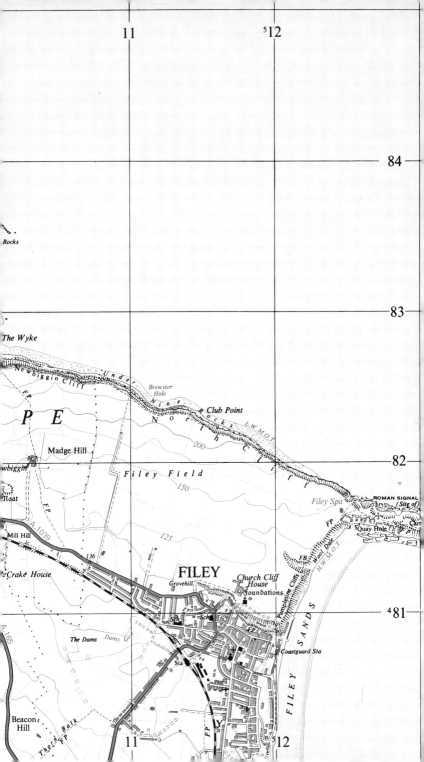

Places of special interest

For Wayfarers fortunate enough to have time to explore the attractive Cleveland countryside, here is a brief summary of the major points of interest on or near to the Way.

Arncliffe Hall

A fine well-preserved Georgian mansion built by Carr of York in the 1750s. The adjoining church has fourteenth century glass and two stone figures of the same period.

Boulby Cliff

The highest point (660 feet) on the English coast, showing huge scars of the alum workings. The view from the radio beacon is one of the finest in Yorkshire.

Byland Abbey

Reached by easy woodland walk from Kilburn White Horse or Rievaulx. The foundation was moved in the twelfth century from Old Byland because its bells confused the monks of Rievaulx. Fine arches and tessellated pavements.

Cringle Moor

A stone seat and bronze memorial plaque indicating principal peaks visible from this magnificent viewpoint.

Easby Moor

Monument to Captain Cook.

Fyling Thorpe

The "Old Hall" just above Boggle Hole Youth Hostel

is the seventeenth-century home of the Cholmleys, defenders of Scarborough Castle against the Parliamentarians.

Guisborough

Austin Priory founded by Robert de Brus about 1119. The present chancel arch comes from the fourteenth century church. In the parish church close by is the magnificent Brus cenotaph.

Hawsker

The church has fine examples of Norse cross and bird figures.

Helmsley

Fine market square with two crosses. Castle founded by Walter L'Espec (The Magnificent) in the early years of the twelfth century. Later additions illustrate developments in military architecture. Access to Duncombe Park and the magnificent terrace above Rievaulx is at east end of the market square.

Kettleness

Still standing are walls of the old village near foot of the cliffs where, on the night of 17 December 1829, a landslide carried the houses into the sea. The inhabitants were taken off the crumbling cliffs by the alum carrier *Henry*.

Mount Grace Priory

Lying just below the Cleveland Way, is easily reached by a forestry ride. Founded in 1398 by Thomas Holland, Duke of Surrey, the monks' cells had running water and individual herb gardens. The restored Lady Chapel is just above the Way.

Osmotherley

Legend claims that "Oswy by his mother lay" after the young prince was killed by the collapse of the rock face at Oswy's Burgh, now Roseberry Topping. The little town was centre of the linen industry in the nineteenth century; the "Walk" mill to the south shelters rare ducks on its millpond. The large spinning mill at Cote Garth on Cod Beck was for a while a Youth Hostel.

Osmotherley market place has an interesting cross and a stone table where fish was sold on Sundays after church.

Rievaulx Abbey

The first Cistercian foundation in the north (1132). The magnificent choir, one of the largest in England, is well looked after by the Department of the Environment. A thatched cottage near the village smithy is reputedly the home of Harold Wilson's grandfather.

Robin Hood's Bay

Notable for its striking situation, with the houses poised on the steep cliff face. The shore and cliffs are a geologist's paradise. The hinterland (Fylingdales Moor) has a wealth of ancient dykes, burial mounds and standing stones, including the famous "Robin Hood's Butts".

Runswick Bay

Similar situation to Robin Hood's Bay. Good off-shore fishing and sailing.

Saltburn

Established by the North Eastern Railway as a holiday resort. The Italian Gardens and the broad, firm sands are the main attractions of one of industrial Teesside's growing dormitory towns.

Staithes

A picturesque fishing village where Captain Cook served as a grocer's apprentice. The high-prowed fishing cobles are built to a Viking pattern. Knitting enthusiasts may like to compare the pattern of fishermen's jerseys in Staithes with those of Runswick, Robin Hood's Bay, Whitby and Filey.

Whorlton

Situated on a "whorl" (conical) hill, about a mile to the north of the Way. You can see a gatehouse of a former Meynell castle and a series of entrenchments which enclosed the medieval village and market. The church has carved effigies from about 1400.

Harry Totcombe

Other information

Youth Hostels on or near the Cleveland Way

		O.S. grid reference
Boggle Hole	Boggle Hole, Fyling Thorpe, Whitby	NZ954040
Helmsley	Carlton Lane, Helmsley, Yorks	SE616840
Saltburn	Riftswood Hall, Victoria Road, Saltburn-by-sea	NZ662206
Scarborough	Burniston Road, Scarborough	SE026907
Westerdale Hall	Westerdale, Whitby	NZ662059
Wheeldale	Wheeldale Lodge, Goathland, Whitby	SE813983
Whitby	East Cliff, Whitby	NZ902111

National Park Warden

R. Bell, Sutherland Cottage, Cropton, Pickering, Yorks. Tel. Lastingham 303.

Rescue Teams

Scarborough Search and Rescue Team: H. Benton, 2 Mount Pleasant, Scarborough. Tel. Scarborough 2530. Cleveland Search and Rescue Team: B. Snowdon, Weavers Cottage, Broughton, near Teesside. Tel. Wainstones 462.

Ramblers' Association (North Yorks Area)

Catering Secretary: Miss P. Bastow, 1 Windsor Road, Redcar, Teesside.
Footpaths Secretary: A. Falconer, 10 Newham Avenue, Middlesbrough, Teesside. Tel. Middlesbrough 85932.

The Country Code

Guard against all risk of fire

Fasten all gates

Keep dogs under proper control

Keep to the paths across farm land

Avoid damaging fences, hedges and walls

Leave no litter

Safeguard water supplies

Protect wild life, wild plants and trees

Go carefully on country roads

Respect the life of the countryside

Bibliography

Charm of the Hambletons, E. Bogg. Miles, Leeds. 1926.
The Cleveland Way, Bill Cowley. Dalesman Publishing Co. Ltd. 1969.
History of the North Riding, William Edwards. Bellows. 1924.
Early Man in North-East Yorkshire, Frank Elgee. Bellows. 1930.
Archaeology of Yorkshire, Frank Elgee. Methuen. 1933.
Walking in Cleveland, Alan Falconer. Dalesman Publishing Co. Ltd. 1966.
The Green Popinjays, Eleanor Fairbairn. Hodder & Stoughton. 1962.
Geology of the Yorkshire Coast, J. E. Hemingway. Geologists' Association Guide 34.
Yorkshire's Ruined Castles, J. L. Illingworth. S. R. Publications. 1970.
The Agriculture of Yorkshire, W. Harwood Long. Royal Agricultural Society. 1970.
Climate and the British Scene, G. Manley. Collins. 1952.
Notes on North-East Weather, G. Manley. Royal Meteorological Society. 1935.
Yorkshire, North Riding, A. J. Mee. Hodder & Stoughton. 1941.
The Ravenscar Nature Trail. North York Moors Park Planning Committee. 1969.
North York Moors National Park, A. Raistrick (Ed.). H.M.S.O. 1966.
Place Names of the North Riding. A. H. Smith. C.U.P. 1928.
Yorkshire, North Riding, Victoria County History. Constable. 1925.
The Old Straight Track, Alfred Watkins. Methuen. 1928.

Scarborough harbour